The Whole-Brain Child Workbook

Practical Exercises, Worksheets and Activities
To Nurture Developing Minds

Daniel J. Siegel, M.D., *and*
Tina Payne Bryson, PH.D.

Published by
PESI Publishing & Media
3839 White Ave
Eau Claire, WI 54703
Printed in the United States of America

ISBN: 978-1-9361287-4-7

LIBRARY OF CONGRESS CATALOGING-IN-PUBLICATION DATA
Siegel, Daniel J., 1957-
    The whole-brain child workbook : practical exercises, worksheets and activities to nurture developing minds / Daniel J. Siegel, M.D. & Tina Payne Bryson, Ph.D.
    pages cm
ISBN 978-1-936128-74-7 (alk. paper) 1. Parenting. 2. Child development. 3. Child psychology. 4. Child rearing. I. Bryson, Tina Payne. II. Title.
  HQ755.8.S53275 2015
  306.874--dc23   2015000374

Illustrations by Tuesday Mourning
Layout Design: Matt Pabich
Cover Design: Amy Rubenzer

PESI
Publishing
& Media
www.pesipublishing.com

Contents

A MESSAGE FROM DAN AND TINA:

We want to express our profound admiration that you've decided to even open this book. We're both parents, so we know how hard it is sometimes just to get through a day, much less read a book about parenting. And now, you've decided not only to read a book about parenting, but to explore a workbook about a book about parenting! We greatly respect the commitment you're making to nurture your children and the health of your family—as well as yourself.

We've written this workbook for you: the busy, possibly overwhelmed but still committed parent who wants to understand at an even deeper level what it means to connect with your children. Maybe you're reading it on your own, or as a part of a group. Maybe you're not even technically a parent, but you want to better understand and relate to the kids you care about. Maybe you are a parent educator and you're using this book to lead a group to greater insight and application of the Whole-Brain approach. Whatever your situation, this workbook is for you.

In the following pages, where we ask you to write, we ask for only a few lines' worth. (You can of course write more if you'd like.) Writing things down is a proven way to deepen and broaden your understanding, and it's a great way to make sense of what you've been doing and how you might consider doing things even better. We've given you various activities you can do on your own and/or with your kids, but these are absolutely optional. We've written the workbook so that each chapter builds on the previous one, but it's fine to skip around.

In other words, there are no absolute rules here. This isn't an additional obligation hanging over your head, or something for you to feel guilty about not doing on a regular basis, or not doing well enough. This workbook is simply a way for you to find more help and support to do what you want to do anyway: move towards a deeper understanding of and connection with your children, and a fuller understanding of yourself as a parent.

Thanks for letting us be a part of your journey.

Dan and Tina

CHAPTER 1

Parenting With The Brain In Mind

*We aren't held captive for the rest of our lives by the way the
brain works at this moment – we can actually rewire it so that
we can be healthier and happier. This is true not only
for children and adolescents, but also for each
of us across the life span.*

– The Whole-Brain Child

In the Introduction to *The Whole-Brain Child*, we discuss the two goals that practically all parents share. The first, most immediate objective, is simply to survive the countless challenging moments we face throughout the day as we interact with our children. Sometimes it feels like that's all we can hope for: to simply survive.

But of course, we want to aim for more than mere survival. We also want our kids to thrive. We want to give them experiences that help them become better human beings, who know what it means to love and trust, to be responsible, to be resilient during difficult times, and to live meaningfully. We want to help them thrive.

Think about these goals as you begin this workbook. Get quiet within yourself, then read the following questions. Once you've had a minute to consider them, write your answers on the lines below. Be as clear and honest as you can. You can think of this book as a personal journal, only for you.

How often, in the course of a day, do you find yourself simply trying to survive a difficult moment with your kids? Think about sibling conflict, behavior issues, homework or screen time battles, disrespect, getting everyone ready in the morning, or anything else. Circle your answer:

1-2 times a day   *3-5 times a day*   *More than 5 times a day*

Now think about those specific survival moments. Many parents typically respond to these challenging situations by focusing primarily on short-term survival. What are your "go-to" survival techniques? Do you yell? Do you separate your kids? Do you offer some sort of incentive (a treat or an opportunity) if behavior changes? Do you threaten them? Give consequences? Make a list of survival techniques you typically depend on:

_____

_____

_____

_____

_____

_____

_____

Now shift your focus, and think about your goals when it comes to helping your children thrive. What do you really want for them, both now and as they move towards adolescence and adulthood? Maybe it has to do with enjoying successful relationships, or living a life full of meaning and significance. Maybe it's about being happy, or independent, or successful. Write about your "thrive goals" for your children. When you think of the people they're going to become, what values are most important to you?

_____

_____

_____

_____

_____

_____

_____

_____

_____

_____

One of our goals with *The Whole-Brain Child* is to help parents recognize that survival moments are also opportunities to help kids thrive. We can take difficult parenting situations and use them to teach our kids the valuable lessons we want them to learn. As we explain in the introduction to *The Whole-Brain Child*, "What's great about this 'survive and thrive' approach is that you don't have to try to carve out special time to help your children thrive. You can use all of the interactions you share—the stressful, angry ones as well as the miraculous, adorable ones—as opportunities to help them become the responsible, caring, capable people you want them to be. To help them be more themselves, more at ease in the world, filled with more resilience and strength. That's what this book is about: using your everyday moments with your kids to help them truly become the people they have the potential to be."

Take a minute now and think about a specific moment from that last few days when something didn't go right between you and one of your kids. Imagine yourself in that moment. Picture yourself, and picture your child. Now write. First, describe your actions and reactions to the situation. Just explain what you did, without emotions of judgment. Imagine that you are a camera recording what happened. (For example, you might write, "When he hit his sister I got SO mad. I didn't yell at him, but I came down hard on him and told him he's too big and too old to be doing that. I basically shamed him. Then I ....")

Write about your experience here.

_____

_____

_____

_____

_____

_____

_____

_____

Now apply the "survive and thrive" model to that situation. When you look at your reaction, to what extent were you simply trying to survive whatever was going wrong in that moment? And to what extent did your actions lead to helping your child thrive and learn important lessons to use in the future? Remember, both goals are important. There's nothing wrong with surviving the moment. The question here is about how much you were also paying attention to building long-term skills and helping your child grow and learn from the experience. Write about that here.

_____

_____

_____

_____

_____

_____

_____

_____

_____

Again, all parents face situations they simply have to survive. It's extremely difficult to raise children, and sometimes the best we can do is just get through the moment. But these experiences will be *so* much more valuable if, instead of merely trying to get through the moment, we *also* seize the opportunity to teach our children about love, respect, empathy, forgiveness, and the other lessons we want to impart to them.

You'll remember the importance we put on the concept of integration. Because there are many different parts to a person's brain, and because each part has different jobs, we need all the parts to work as an integrated whole in order for us to function at our best.

As parents, we want to help our children become better integrated so they can use their entire brain in a coordinated way. When all the areas of your child's brain are working together, she experiences a sense of integration and thriving. For example, you may notice that during those times of integration she can much better handle any setbacks, and disappointments can be more calmly managed since she has the patience and insight to be able to work through her frustrations.

In those moments, she's neither rigid nor chaotic. She's in the river of wellbeing.

The rest of this workbook will help you focus more specifically on ways to view "survive moments" as opportunities to help your children thrive. Often, the focus will be on helping you improve your own capacity to remain in the river of wellbeing. And at times we'll discuss how to do the same for your kids. Along the way, we'll give you numerous opportunities to go deeper with the ideas from *The Whole-Brain Child* and to apply those concepts in ways that will help your kids, yourself, and your whole family survive, as well as thrive.

HOW TO USE THIS WORKBOOK

We envision that you will use this workbook individually, by reading it and writing in it on your own. But we've also designed it with groups in mind. Certain clinicians and educators may lead groups of individuals who work through the concepts on their own, then come together and share what they discovered for themselves. Or even if you're not a professional, feel free to gather friends and fellow caregivers to discuss what you each discover as you explore the ideas we've included here. Sharing and examining these concepts with others will only deepen your understanding of them and help you apply them in ways that make your relationship with your kids that much more meaningful and significant.

You'll find too that we've included here many different activities and exercises you can enjoy with your children. In doing so, you can teach them about their own brains, and help them understand basic concepts around the subject of integration (even if you never use the word), and thus prepare them to be better human beings, and better relationship partners as they grow into adolescence and adulthood. What's more, you'll strengthen the bond you share with them and teach them important skills that will not only help you survive the difficult parenting moments throughout the day, but also help them thrive and become happier, healthier, and more fully themselves.

Two Brains are Better Than One

*Using only the right or left brain would be like trying to swim
using only one arm. We might be able to do it, but wouldn't we
be a lot more successful – and avoid going in circles –
if we used both arms together?*

– The Whole-Brain Child

How do you typically respond to your kids when they're upset? For some parents, their "go-to" is to respond with their left-brain and just focus on facts and solutions. Do these phrases sound familiar?

Don't worry. There's nothing to be afraid of.

It's not a big deal that it broke. Just fix it.

There's no reason to cry. Losing is part of the game.

Homework is your job. Just get it done. If you focus, you'll be finished sooner.

There's nothing inherently wrong with offering a logic-based response—except that it rarely works when a child is upset. Left-brain logic is almost never effective when a child is in the middle of a right-brain meltdown. Does that ring true with your own kids?

Other parents may react from the right brain. The good news in this instance is that it provides the chance for emotional connection. The danger, though, is that by responding entirely from an emotional place ourselves, we risk flooding our child with more chaos and are unable to offer the sort of attuned response he needs to safely experience his own emotions.

Left Hemisphere	Right Hemisphere
Logical	Able to sense emotions and information from the body
Linear	Non-linear
Linguistic	Nonverbal
Literal	Can put things in context and see the whole picture

The key, of course, as we explain in *The Whole-Brain Child*, is to *integrate* the two sides of the brain, allowing them to work together as a team. We don't want to be working from only a left-brained perspective—which would result in an emotional desert—or solely from a right-brained perspective—which can produce an emotional tsunami. Neither one by itself for long periods of time is good. But when both sides work together, and we approach our children from a Whole-Brain perspective, then we can much more fully meet their needs and help guide them back into the River of Wellbeing.

To help you feel clear about the difference between right-mode and left-mode processing, try this brief exercise. Take a moment to pause and reflect on the experience of your child's birth, or the first time you held your adopted baby, or some other significant moment in your life.

Let's do that now. Close your eyes, be still, and remember that event. Give yourself time to get back into the experience, and swim in that memory for a few moments. Then open your eyes and proceed.

If you thought about the event in a linear way without much emotion or bodily sensations, you'd be in a left-brain mode. In that case, your story might go something like this:

> *Well, first my contractions began, then we called the doctor and headed to the hospital. The nurses gave me an epidural. The doctor came at 2pm and our son was born 75 minutes later. My parents came into the room, and ....*

Is this how you remembered the event when you closed your eyes? Probably not. In fact, very few people recall meaningful, significant events that way.

More often, people remember important experiences in more of a right-brain mode, where different images from that memory come up in what sometimes feels like a non-linear, almost random way, maybe even accompanied by bodily sensations and emotions that emerge as they remember. Does that sound more like how you recollected your event?

In many ways, it's similar to waking from a dream: It's not logical, events don't make sense, you might still feel emotional, and you may experience heaviness, sadness, elation, or even anger in your body, much as you did at the original event. This way of remembering is more of a right-brain way of processing memories.

But to really understand life, you can't use just one mode or the other. You need both the left and right brain, where the left brain gives words and order and the right brain gives emotional textures and context to your experiences. In other words, you want to integrate both modes of processing as much as possible.

The same goes for your kids, especially when they're upset and not controlling their emotions and body.

How do your kids signal to you that they're having a hard time?

Take a minute now and describe what happens when your child is experiencing an emotional tsunami. What does she look like? What does she do? Is there crying? Screaming? Does she throw objects? As you look through the list of common responses below, circle the ones that most often apply to your child. And feel free to add your own if your child has her own unique way of freaking out! If you have more than one child, you can write each child's list on a separate piece of paper so it's easier to focus on each child, individually.

- Screaming
- Crying
- Throwing things
- Hitting
- Lashing out, verbally (*"I hate you!"* or *"You're so mean."*)
- Whining

- Hurting self, physically
- Seething anger
- Hurting others, physically
- Refusal to communicate
- Slamming doors
- Sulking
- Sarcasm

- Flushed face
- Clenched fists
- Stomping feet
- Rolling eyes
- Loss of language (*groans, grunts...*)
- Physical complaints (*stomach aches, headaches...*)

Now that you're thinking about how your child most commonly expresses her highest level of emotional intensity, take a few minutes to list any additional details that may help you paint a full picture of her during these events.

_____

_____

_____

_____

_____

_____

_____

_____

_____

_____

_____

_____

_____

_____

_____

It's understandable that you'd want to focus on ending meltdowns or tantrums like these, as well as other behaviors that seem irrational and overblown. However, looking at the lists above, do you see any of your child's difficult behaviors that could be interpreted as simply signals that let you know she's no longer able to regulate her behavior? That her brain is "NONintegrated," or what, at an extreme, can feel "DISintegrated"?

That's what many of the behaviors you listed are: *messages* that your child sends to let you know that her brain isn't in a state of integration, and that she needs help building skills when it comes to handling challenging situations.

So now that you're aware of *her* signals, let's reflect on how you can lead the way to re-integration.

HOW DO YOU RESPOND WHEN YOUR KIDS ARE UPSET?

Think about yourself now, and how you respond in high-stress situations with your kids. When you see the signs you described above, what's *your* response? Do you generally respond with logic, explaining the reasons behind why your child shouldn't feel like she does? Do you typically match emotion with emotion, elevating the chaos in the situation? Or are you usually more integrated, combining left- and right-brain approaches? If you're like most parents, it depends on the day!

Most likely you react differently depending on the circumstances, but, on the whole, how do you typically respond? Below, circle the number that most corresponds to your typical response when your child is emotionally flooded.

0	1	2	3	4	5	6	7	8	9	10
Left-brain					Integration					Right-brain
Emotional desert										Emotional tsunami

Now, in the space below, go deeper with that thought. Write, for example, about what triggers your reaction. How does your body feel when your child explodes emotionally? What goes through your mind during the tsunami? How do you feel after the wave has passed? Are you more left-brained or right-brained in your response? *There are no right or wrong answers here.* This is just a chance for you to get clear on your own experience in these moments.

So just take a minute to relax, picture the situation if that's helpful to you, then write.

_____

_____

_____

_____

_____

_____

_____

_____

_____

_____

_____

_____

One of the main purposes of this chapter in the workbook is to allow you to get clear on how you typically respond to your children when they are struggling emotionally, and to help you think through how *you* feel about your typical response to their needs. Being aware of your approach allows you to make changes when they're necessary.

Once you're aware of your *own* typical response, not only do you have more opportunities for modeling the sort of behavior you want your child to exhibit, but you're also more capable of connecting with your child in the way he needs to bring his brain back to a state of integration.

Whole-Brain Strategy #1:
Connect And Redirect

We've heard many parents tell us that our Connect and Redirect strategy works like magic when it comes to helping them achieve their survive goal of getting through a difficult moment, as well as their long-term thrive goal of helping their children become resilient, kind, respectful, and happy people.

You'll remember that the Connect and Redirect strategy contains two steps:

Step 1: Connect with the Right

When your child is upset, logic often won't work until we've responded to the right brain's emotional needs. Acknowledging feelings in a nonjudgmental way, using physical touch, empathetic facial expressions, and a nurturing tone of voice, are all ways you use your right brain to connect. By starting with this act of attunement, you allow your child to "feel felt" before you begin trying to solve problems or address the situation.

Step 2: Redirect with the Left

Once you sense that your child's brain has settled enough that it can handle a left-brain, logical approach, you can then redirect by problem-solving with your child or making suggestions on what he can do now that he's feeling calmer and more in control of himself.

Connect with the Right	Redirect with the Left
Touch	Solutions
Tone of Voice	Words
Facial Expression	Planning
Empathy	Logical explanations
Pausing	Setting boundaries

WHAT CONNECTING DOES *NOT* LOOK LIKE

Where we most often see Connect and Redirect go awry is when parents become triggered by their child's tone of voice or "irrational" demands, so the parents are less able to connect with real attunement. As a result, their *words* sound like they're connecting, but the overall response doesn't feel warm and nurturing.

For example, do you ever hear yourself saying, "I can tell you're really mad right now," but you say it with tone of irritation or like a robot instead of warmth? Or have you caught yourself frowning, hands on hips, as you say, "I know you're mad at me, but I told you to hurry three times!" Connection requires more than just kind words or an acknowledgement of an emotion. The overall *feel* of the interaction needs to be full of warmth and affection for connection to occur. Our goal is for him to "feel felt" and experience that we "get" what he's feeling. We want him to *know* that we're there for him.

STRATEGY #1
INSTEAD OF COMMAND AND DEMAND...

...TRY CONNECT AND REDIRECT

Take a moment now and think about times your child has been upset, and you offered a response *without* connection. In a minute we'll ask you to explore this idea further. For now, just think about a couple of examples of when you could have been more warm and nurturing when your child needed it. List them here.

_____

_____

_____

_____

_____

_____

_____

_____

_____

It's important to remember that often, in those difficult moments, our child is not simply giving us a hard time – rather, she is *having* a hard time and needs our help to re-integrate her brain.

WHAT ARE YOUR NONVERBALS?

As we discussed in *The Whole-Brain Child*, nonverbal communication plays a big role in the Connect and Redirect strategy. Many of us use this type of communication automatically, without giving it much thought. But again, when our nonverbal communication isn't in sync with our verbal communication, it can be very confusing for children.

Think about all the ways you use nonverbal communication with your child when he's emotionally overwhelmed. Consider that your own behaviors might aid or hinder connection with your child depending on how you approach each situation.

In the graph below, we've listed eight different types of nonverbal communication we all use on a daily basis. In an effort to more deeply understand how the subtleties of these behaviors can affect our kids, give some thought to how different approaches might result in created or lost connection with your kids.

In the boxes, briefly describe what each version of nonverbal communication says to your child. You can ask yourself questions like: If I do it this way, how does my child view me? How does she view herself? How might communicating this way make my child feel that I understand her (or don't understand her)? We've provided an example in the first line to give you an idea of how small changes in your behavior can make a huge difference.

Creating Connection	Losing Connection
Eye Contact: *Getting down to my child's level (or better yet, below his level) and looking into his eyes while I talk to him helps him feel safe and that I am not a threatening presence.*	**Eye Contact:** *Standing over him while I look down at him makes me look huge and imposing. Whatever I say from this position communicates threat to him, and he automatically wants to defend himself.*
Facial Expression *(example: "soft" eyes, relaxed face…)*	**Facial Expression** *(example: frown, pursed lips, aggressive looks…)*
Tone of Voice (example: soft, comforting, calm…)	**Tone of Voice** (example: tense, loud, angry…)
Posture (example: relaxed shoulders, open hands, perhaps kneeling…)	**Posture** (example: arms crossed, hands on hips, leaning forward…)
Gestures (example: gentle touches, offering hugs…)	**Gestures** (example: wagging finger, throwing arms up in the air…)
Timing of response (example: letting child finish before speaking, asking questions before answering…)	**Timing of Response** (example: interrupting, long intimidating pauses…)
Intensity of response (example: staying calm, being patient…)	**Intensity of Response** (example: yelling, crying, big intensity…)
Bodily Movement (example: coming closer, relaxed movement, bending down…)	**Bodily Movement** (example: walking away quickly, stomping, jerky movement…)

Children are incredibly perceptive of everything – especially our reactions towards them. In working through this exercise you're making *yourself more* aware of how many nonverbal ways you communicate with your child, and how each of them can impact how connected or how reactive your child feels toward you in a given moment.

Still, it can be hard at times to parent the way we intend to – especially when our children's behaviors seem irrational, or the solution to their problem seems obvious. It's in these moments where we often make the mistake of trying to redirect or solve *before we* connect – fixing problems without noticing feelings or offering empathy.

However, understanding what that feels like when it happens can help you avoid making that mistake with your child. The following reflection is designed to do just that.

How do you want to be responded to when you're upset?

Think back to a recent experience where you were upset and having a hard time dealing with something. It might have had to do with your kids, or maybe something happened at work or you experienced conflict with someone in your life.

Now, imagine you went to someone you care about – a close friend or your significant other – and told that person how upset you were. Imagine that when you did, this person argued with you, or told you that you shouldn't be upset, or tried to distract you, or said you were just tired or should stop making such a big deal about it.

Sit with that response for a minute. Tune in to how your body feels. Does your jaw feel tight? Do tears well up? What might you want to say in response? Do you argue back? Do you shut down or want to withdraw? Do you feel as though this is a person you can trust the next time you're upset? Do you feel safe and supported? Or very much alone? Write about your thoughts and responses:

_____

_____

_____

_____

_____

Now visualize the same recent situation, but this time, imagine that the person you turned to offered you connection. In this circumstance you're listened to and soothed, validated, and even if the problem isn't solved, the response allows you to calm down so you can begin addressing the issue for yourself. Write about what you imagine you would feel, think, and experience in this second scenario:

_____

_____

_____

_____

_____

As you've probably noticed, having someone minimize your problem or tell you how to solve it, when what you really want is empathy, is a pretty straight road to feeling disconnected from them and feeling more reactive!

Obviously, we want our kids to experience the more connection-focused response, but it's not always what happens. As a parent it's impossible not to get frustrated at times, but being more aware of what makes you lose connection will allow you to make small changes in your response, and that can have a big effect on *your* child's reaction.

WHAT KEEPS YOU FROM CONNECTING?

So, if we have the intention to be connected parents, what is it that keeps us from being able to do it all the time? The answers to that can be complex and varied. Let's take a look at what the answers are for you.

First, think about anything that prevents you from connecting with your child. Do any of these ring true for you?

- Your lack of sleep

- A fear of reinforcing bad behavior

- Expecting too much of your child at his or her age

- Discomfort with being judged by family members or strangers (having them think you're overly harsh or permissive)

- Feeling overwhelmed by other commitments (to be on time, to follow a plan, to care for your other children ....)

These are just examples that prevent connection for most parents from time to time. What else would you add to the list? To put it differently, think about the last time your child was upset and your response left you two feeling disconnected from each other and even more upset. Write about the cause—or causes—of that disconnection. Remember, focus right now on *your own* response to the situation, not on your child's behavior.

_____

_____

_____

_____

_____

_____

_____

Acknowledging all of the ways our hectic lives and our own sensitivities get in the way of our goals can be an eye-opening experience for many parents. We often blame ourselves or feel guilty for not being able to do what we think we should be doing, without understanding the complex reasons behind *why* we were unable to do what we intended.

The reflections you've just completed required you to look deeply at many subtle emotions and reactions you may not have been consciously aware of before. That's a lot of hard work on your part! Take a minute to acknowledge that, and to congratulate yourself for being so honest with yourself.

With this focused insight now part of your tool box, let's move forward and combine it with the Connect and Redirect strategy using examples from your family situations.

IMAGINING CONNECTION

Let's begin with a hypothetical example to set the scene. In the first column of the following chart, we've given you a parenting dilemma you might face, where a child is excited about going on a sleepover and you've made your own plans. But when it comes time to leave, she refuses to go because she says she's afraid of sleeping away from home.

In the second column we've given a typical parental response, which is focused not on connection, but instead on pushing *the parent's* agenda. The child's response to this method is described in the third column.

The fourth column gives an idea of what real connection would look like, where a parent allows the child to feel felt and listened to, and then how the parent would move towards redirection. The fifth column shows what the child's reaction to this would likely be.

We've then left you some boxes for you to fill in with your own scenarios. In the first column think of an actual situation you've faced with one of your own kids. Then write how you've typically responded, and how you might have been able to handle it better if you'd focused on connecting *before* redirecting. Put yourself in your child's shoes and fill in how they may have felt, and how they would respond to your different approaches.

Scenario where child gets upset	Typical parental response	What child may experience/do	What connect and redirect would look like	What child may experience/do
Child excited about sleepover, but at last minute doesn't want to go.	"What?! But you're dying to go on this sleepover!" Or "Oh, you'll be fine! You'll have a great time!"	Feeling dismissed and that parents are denying and minimizing my feelings. Shut down and refuse to go.	Pull child close; take deep breath, say, "Sounds like you're having some second thoughts." Validate feelings, then problem solve.	Feeling understood and supported. Able to calm down and talk through worries about being afraid.

Scenario where child gets upset	Typical parental response	What child may experience/do	What connect and redirect would look like	What child may experience/do

The more you witness your child responding positively to the Connect and Redirect strategy, the more likely you will be to use it. And the more you practice using it, the more it will become one of your default responses when your child is having a hard time.

You may find it helpful to go back through these reflections as your familiarity with Connect and Redirect deepens to see if you still get stuck in certain areas. But for now, let's move on to the next Whole-Brain Strategy.

Whole-Brain Strategy #2:
Name It to Tame It

For small children, it's not only a "big-T" trauma like a car accident or the death of a grandparent that can feel overwhelming and unnerving. So can a "little-t" trauma, like falling down at the playground or losing a favorite stuffed animal. Big emotions and bodily sensations can flood your child's right brain, keeping him from calming down or leaving him stuck in his fear.

As parents, it can be tempting to brush things off or gloss over certain events – particularly those that seem small to us ("Stop crying. You're fine!"). Instead, when we recall the "Name It to Tame It" strategy, we remember that using storytelling helps our child calm her flooded right brain and access her logical left-brain to explain and put things in order after a traumatic (or Traumatic) event.

STRATEGY #2
INSTEAD OF DISMISS AND DENY...

...TRY NAME IT TO TAME IT

The stories our children need include both left-brain logic and words, as well as the right-brain's ability to sense emotion, context, and meaning, so we can lead them back to a state where they're able to problem solve, strategize, and feel a sense of empowerment over the situation.

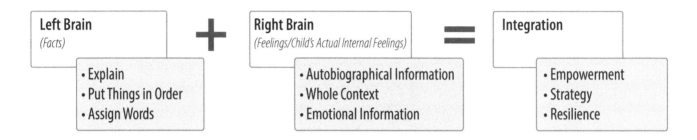

WHICH WAY DOES YOUR BRAIN LEAN?

Remember at the beginning of the chapter when we asked whether you typically respond with primarily a left- or right-brained approach when your child is upset? Let's give some thought at this point to how left- or right-brain dominant you are.

In your life outside of parenting, do you ever focus on just facts and talk strategies, without acknowledging feelings? Do you tend to go into fix-it mode when presented with problems? If so, you're probably likely to approach with a more left-brained mode.

On the other hand, do you find yourself often flooded with emotion in response to internal and external situations? Are you able to empathize with others and match their emotions with your own—sometimes even beyond what's healthy and helpful? In that case, you're most likely operating predominantly from a right-brained mode.

Take a minute and explore this question. In your life as a whole, are you typically more left- or right-brained?

_____

_____

_____

_____

_____

_____

_____

WHAT HAS INFLUENCED YOUR RESPONSES
TO YOUR CHILDREN'S EMOTIONS?

Now think about where your typical responses may have come from. When you think about your own childhood, how were feelings handled in your family? Were your emotions dismissed or shamed by your parents so that you learned to hide them whenever they began to emerge? Or, in contrast, did your caregivers live in the middle of an emotional tsunami, so that you at times needed shelter from the storm of their emotions?

What do you remember about what did and didn't work in terms of how your caregivers responded to your childhood emotions? Detail your memories here:

_____

_____

_____

_____

_____

_____

_____

_____

Now compare the ways you were responded to when you were upset as a child, with how you respond to your own kids when they are struggling. Our own experiences from childhood ultimately affect our parenting approach with our own children. As adults, we often find ourselves either wanting to do things differently from how our parents did, or following our parents' examples. Our children's behaviors can bring up many unresolved emotions for us that, at times, may get in the way of parenting the way we want to.

What similarities do you notice between your own and your parents' responses to big emotions? And where do you differ from how you were parented when difficult moments came up?

_____

_____

_____

_____

_____

_____

_____

This exploration of your own feelings and experiences is extremely important—for you as well as your kids. *In fact, the best predictor of how well children turn out in terms of their attachment is how their parents have made sense of their own history as expressed in how they tell their life story.* These narratives can reveal how we each have mental models, or schema, of how relationships are supposed to work. These models are based on past relationships and determine how we function in current relationships with our significant others, family, friends, and children.

So the more we reflect on and understand ourselves now, and our histories in the past with our own parents, the better we can understand why we're responding the way we do to our children. (By the way, this idea is central to Dan's book *Parenting From the Inside Out,* written with Mary Hartzell. That's a good resource if you're interested in exploring these concepts more fully and learning to make sense of your own life story.)

HOW SUPPORTED DO YOU FEEL AS A PARENT?

As you attempt to connect with your kids, and be more nurturing and responsive when they're having a hard time, do you feel supported in this effort by the other adults in the life of your children? Think about your significant other, your parents, your in-laws, and anyone else. How much do you feel that you're a part of a team of caregivers, all working to provide consistent, loving care to your children?

_____

_____

_____

_____

_____

_____

Depending on what you've written here, you may want to explore these ideas with the other caregivers in your child's life. Becoming aware of our various feelings toward our children's emotional and behavioral difficulties is an important step toward being able to attune without coloring the moment with our own emotional reactions and needs.

WHOLE-BRAIN KIDS

As you know, _The Whole-Brain Child_ features several "Whole-Brain Kids" illustrations to help parents teach their children some of the key concepts in the book. One in particular focuses on how kids' brains become flooded with emotion, and why storytelling and talking through difficult moments can be so calming.

We've reproduced it here so you can read it with your own kids.

YOUR LEFT BRAIN AND YOUR RIGHT BRAIN

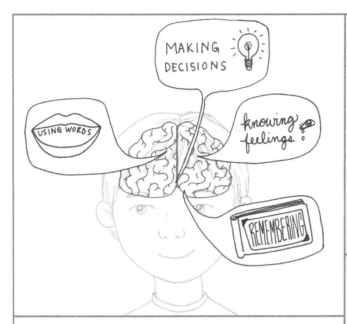

DO YOU KNOW THAT YOU HAVE MANY PARTS TO YOUR BRAIN AND THEY ALL DO DIFFERENT THINGS? IT'S ALMOST LIKE YOU HAVE DIFFERENT BRAINS WITH MINDS OF THEIR OWN. BUT WE CAN HELP THEM ALL GET ALONG AND HELP ONE ANOTHER.

OUR RIGHT BRAIN LISTENS TO OUR BODY AND OTHER PARTS OF OUR BRAIN AND KNOWS ABOUT OUR BIG FEELINGS LIKE WHEN WE'RE HAPPY, OR BRAVE, OR SCARED, OR SAD, OR REALLY MAD. IT'S IMPORTANT THAT WE PAY ATTENTION TO THESE FEELINGS AND TALK ABOUT THEM.

SOMETIMES WHEN WE'RE UPSET AND WE DON'T TALK ABOUT IT, OUR FEELINGS CAN BUILD AND BUILD INSIDE US, LIKE A HUGE WAVE THAT WASHES OVER US AND MAKES US SAY OR DO THINGS WE DON'T MEAN.

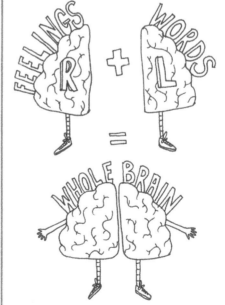

BUT THE LEFT BRAIN CAN HELP PUT OUR FEELINGS INTO WORDS. THEN OUR WHOLE BRAIN CAN WORK TOGETHER AS A TEAM AND WE CAN CALM DOWN.

FOR EXAMPLE:

ANNIE GOT SICK AND HAD TO MISS HER FRIEND'S BIRTHDAY PARTY. SHE WAS SO MAD ABOUT STAYING HOME THAT A HUGE ANGER WAVE GREW AND GREW AND WAS ABOUT TO CRASH DOWN ON HER.

ANNIE'S DAD HELPED HER TALK ABOUT WHAT SHE WAS FEELING.

WHEN SHE USED HER WORDS TO SAY HOW SHE FELT, HER LEFT BRAIN HELPED HER SURF THE BIG ANGER WAVE FROM HER RIGHT BRAIN, AND SHE RODE IT TO SHORE, CALM AND HAPPY.

Putting an upsetting or confusing event into context for a child, and giving her the words to use to access and explain her emotions, helps her access her logical left-brain and calm down her emotional right-brain.

TELL ME A STORY

One of the most helpful ways to walk your child through a difficult event is to tell the story about past or even upcoming events that are causing fear or anxiety. When you are dealing with more long-term fears or concerns, ones that seem to be lingering, creating a storybook can allow you to talk through the events (words from the left brain) and the feelings and interconnections among various aspects of your life (the rich emotions and the context from the right brain) with your child. Doing so can help tame the reactivity of the right hemisphere. It allows you to take an event that may be producing images and strong emotions that the child may not have made sense of, and bring linear language to explain it so that the story becomes an integrated experience.

Making these books can be as simple or complex as you want it to be. Tina made one for her youngest son before he started preschool. Knowing that the first day of school can be scary for a young child, she wanted him to feel as comfortable and at-home as possible when he first entered the classroom. So the two of them visited the school before the first day and took photos of the classrooms, the playground, the teachers – even the bathrooms! Together they put the photos into a simple document that she printed out and bound with string.

In the days that led up to the first day of school, when he would have questions or worries about school, they would read "When J.P. Goes To School." As they looked through each page she read the simple details that accompanied each photo. For example, the first page introduced her son to the idea of preparing for school:

> *Today is a school day for J.P. He gets to go to his own school! He will learn fun things and play with friends. First J.P. gets ready for school. He eats a healthy breakfast. He brushes his teeth, then he picks out his clothes and gets dressed all by himself. He's such a big boy!*

The book continues with specifics about the morning routine and then adds autobiographical information and context to the story while bringing in her son's right-brain feelings and emotions:

> *Sometimes J.P. might be sad when Mom or Dad says goodbye, but he's a brave boy. If he feels sad, he can look at his Dodgers tattoo on his arm to remind him that Mom and Dad will be back soon. He can tell his teachers if he needs help or comfort. Then J.P. will feel better and will play with his friends.*

Towards the end of the book, Tina allowed for her son to experience a sense of mastery and control over his experience:

> *At the end of each day, J.P. will get to come home and tell Mommy, Daddy, and your big brothers about your time at school! We are so excited to hear about your day at school!*

J.P.'s book also included details like what the morning routine at school would look like, what he would do in class during the day, photos of his teachers and the classroom, and what he could look forward to when Mom or Dad picked him up at the end of the day.

It's common for children to be fearful, but not really understand what it is they're afraid of or how to talk about it. We want to be attuned enough to our kids that we can understand their fears and help them put their emotions into words. In doing so we help tame them and integrate them. Sitting with them and reading their book as often as they want can allow our kids to work through their worries—about a new school or Halloween fears or anything else—in a safe place with an adult who can comfort and support him.

If you want to make a book with your own child, just choose an event that's causing her to experience stress, fear, anxiety, pain, or any sort of unhappiness. Maybe it's an upcoming doctor's appointment, or the arrival of a new sibling. Or maybe it's an event from the past that's still troubling her. Remember: what may be an exciting or uneventful experience for you can be the cause of big, negative emotions for your child, and she may not have any idea how to understand or express what's going on within her.

When you make your book, you can use photographs or draw stick figures. You can make it by hand or print it out from your computer. It can have as many pages as you need to tell the story in detail. The way it looks matters less than the content and the emotions you delve into. Simple sentences and a little detective work to understand their mind will make this a book that allows your child to move from struggling in an emotional tsunami to masterfully surfing the waves of her emotions.

The "Name it to Tame It" strategy emphasizes three basic storytelling priorities:

1. The facts. *Cover the left-brain information so that what actually happened can be understood.*

2. Your child's feelings. *Explore your child's internal experience, whatever it is—not just the rosy version that's all sunshine and rainbows.*

3. A message of empowerment. *Give your child something he can do to feel better and attain mastery. This might involve offering some sort of tool to help regulate emotions (like the Dodgers tattoo and a reminder that JP could go talk to his teacher).*

You may find that your child wants to read this book over and over. It may be just what you need to have a conversation about the situation, the feelings about the experience, and the way to empower your child to successfully manage the difficult emotions. From there you can begin to more deeply understand your child and help him reach a place of comfort.

This is the beauty of appealing to our children's left- and right-brain needs with attuned connection. Doing so allows us to be the guide they need to ultimately understand and calm their own emotions.

CHAPTER 3

Building The Staircase of The Mind
Integrating the Upstairs and Downstairs Brain

> *A key goal for any parent should be to help*
> *build and reinforce the metaphorical stairway*
> *that connects the child's upper and lower brain*
> *so that the two can work as a team.*
>
> -*The Whole-Brain Child*

Among the many skills parents hope to teach their children, being able to control impulses, calm big feelings, and make good decisions ranks high on the list. Since the area of the brain that controls these functions doesn't fully develop until people reach their mid-twenties, parents have to teach these skills with some understanding of *what* to teach, *when* to teach, and *how much* their child can understand at any given moment.

You'll recall that in *The Whole-Brain Child* we looked at the brain as a house with an upstairs, a downstairs, and a stairway that connects the two.

The jobs belonging to the downstairs brain are more primitive and often involve basic needs and instincts. The upstairs brain, on the other hand, is more sophisticated and responsible for many of the characteristics and behaviors we hope to see in our kids.

Downstairs Brain	Upstairs Brain
Fight/flight/freeze response	Sound decision making and planning
Autonomic function (breathing, blinking, instincts, …)	Balancing emotions and body
Sensory memories	Self-understanding/reflection
Strong emotions (fear, anger, excitement,…)	Empathy
Acting before thinking	Morality

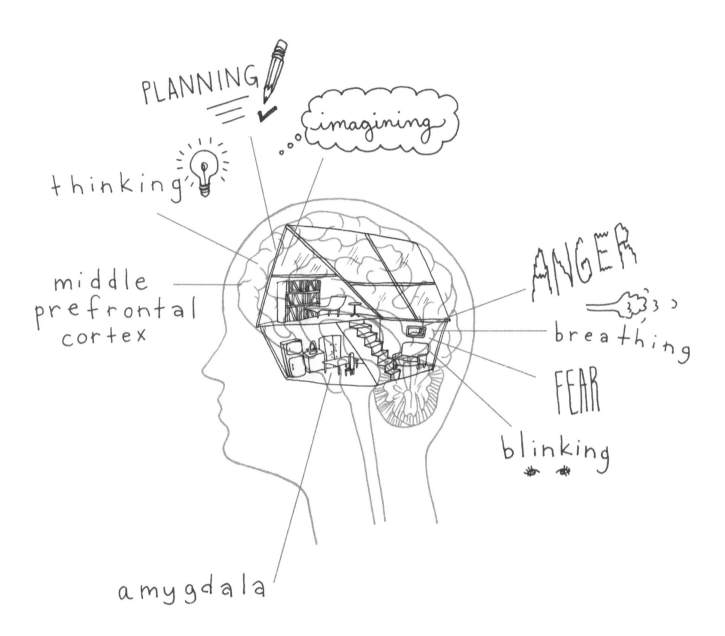

When these two parts of the brain are integrated, a person is able to perform complex tasks such as pausing to consider consequences before acting, considering the feelings of others, and making moral or ethical judgments.

However, we have to remember that this upstairs brain doesn't complete its development until the mid-twenties, which means that it's vulnerable to not working well sometimes. With this in mind, kids and teens can't be expected to exhibit the sort of control over their bodies, emotions, and actions that adults can. Frankly, even with a fully developed upstairs brain, many adults don't have sufficient practice using it and still have difficulty accessing the skills associated with it!

What are your expectations for your kids?

Let's discuss what it means to take an honest inventory of our conscious and nonconscious expectations, in order to make realistic adjustments about what we believe our children are capable of.

When you consider your beliefs about your child and how you respond to him, how much do you blame him for his bad behavior? Are there times you assume that the bad behavior is because of character flaws or because there's something wrong with him or even that he's just choosing not to do the right thing? Do you ever feel as though he really could do better but just doesn't want to?

For example, here's one way to look at a child who refuses to do his homework.

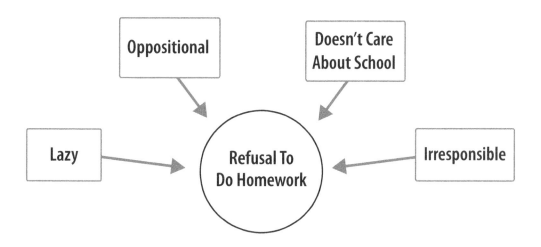

In an effort to look at this behavior with everything we know about the brain, we could also see it this way:

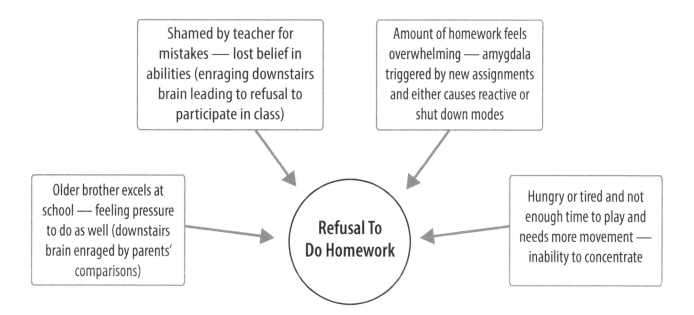

Are there times you expect too much of your child? For younger kids this might have to do with sitting through meals, or sharing, or dealing with a scary situation. For older kids it might have more to do with staying organized or planning ahead with schoolwork, controlling their emotions, managing their anxiety, or being patient with their siblings. List examples of times your expectations might be a bit unreasonable—especially considering that the upstairs brain isn't fully developed—then write a sentence or two explaining each one.

_____

_____

_____

_____

_____

_____

Next, write about specific steps you could take to address your child's behavior, now that you've thought more about your expectations. For example, instead of expecting your two-year-old to sit quietly through a meal without disrupting it, you might have coloring pages or Play Doh® always at the ready. Or you might want to work with your middle-schooler with regular check-ins and on how to use a planner and organize homework assignments. List two or three strategies here.

_____

_____

_____

_____

_____

_____

Now, think about specific steps you can take to support yourself in your new set of expectations. Maybe you ask your partner to agree to help with the changes, or devise a plan for more time in the morning before school to reduce stress, or call to swap childcare with a neighbor. List a few action steps here.

_____

_____

_____

_____

_____

_____

What we've found is that when parents have a better understanding of child development and their child's developing brain and are better able to set realistic and age-appropriate expectations for their kids, the result is a big reduction in power struggles and misbehavior.

By reflecting on what skills your child might not have developed yet, you become better able to understand that when your child is "acting out," it's really a sign that she's having trouble accomplishing what's being asked of her and that she might need help.

This isn't at all to say that you turn a blind eye to misbehavior. In fact, understanding how the upstairs and downstairs brains work gives parents an effective strategy for responding in the heat of the moment – like when your child has a tantrum.

RESPONDING TO TANTRUMS

When tantrums occur – and they will – many parents immediately implement the Command and Demand method: *"Stop fighting right now! Give your sister a turn with the ball!"*

However, approaching a tantrum in this way often triggers your child's downstairs brain and results in a power struggle. Your child won't feel understood, and you'll be teaching him that making demands will enable him to get what he wants.

Discipline in a tantrum moment will be much more effective if you begin by understanding the actual nature of the tantrum, and whether it originates in the upstairs or downstairs regions of the brain.

Upstairs Tantrum Characteristics

• Conscious choice to act out and push buttons
• Strategic, manipulative attempt to control the situation
• Child can be reasoned with, make choices, control her emotions
• Child can instantly stop when her demands are met

> NOTE: Very young children are not capable of having these types of tantrums. they actually don't have the neural structures in place to think like this.

Downstairs Tantrum Characteristics

• Stress hormones flooding the body, interfering with functioning of upstairs brain
• Loss of control over body and emotions, along with a high degree of stress
• Child is incapable of making choices or being reasoned with

As you can see, there are very different processes taking place in your child's body and brain depending on what sort of tantrum she's having. Many of us usually respond automatically when our child flips her lid: we can get triggered and flip our lids as well!

But with a little practice, we can learn to lovingly respond and help calm the situation, rather than just react, when our child is having trouble making good decisions and staying in control of himself.

HOW DO YOU RESPOND TO TANTRUMS?

Think about your customary response to the following situations, being as honest as you can. Take your time imagining each situation below, especially if it's a familiar scenario for you. In addition to what you might do (*negotiating, pleading, giving in…*), also take notice of what sorts of feelings, thoughts, or body sensations come up for you. Does your jaw tighten? Does your heart beat faster? In the right hand column, jot down a few notes about how you might react in moments like these.

There are no wrong answers; you're simply exploring what are often automatic or habitual responses to your child's reactive moments. If you can think of specific tantrums that have come up recently with your own child, feel free to use those in place of the sample ones below.

Tantrum Situation	Your Typical Response
At the park your preschooler gets furious and hits another child who won't share sand toys with him.	
You tell your son to turn off his video game. He gets very angry and tells you he hates you.	
You ask your daughter to stop playing with her toys before dinner but she ignores you. When you insist, she throws her toys across the room, crying.	
Your daughter is getting angrier and angrier as she insists upon getting another new pair of shoes.	
Your son clings to you, crying, as you drop him off at camp.	

Did you find that in some cases you had more patience than in others? Did one kind of tantrum make you more upset than another? Also, how do you talk to yourself when your child tantrums? (*Here we go again. She's always doing this!*) What judgments are you making about who your child is (*He's so spoiled.*)? The more you can get clear on your own feelings here, the more intentionally you can respond to future tantrums. Write about what you notice.

_____

_____

_____

_____

_____

_____

_____

Once you've thought about your own thoughts and the judgments you're making, consider *how effective* your typical response is. Does your typical approach to handling tantrums leave you and your child feeling calm and connected, or furious and worn out and disconnected?

_____

_____

_____

_____

_____

_____

_____

Now write about what you think you could change that would make the experience of responding to your child's tantrums more positive for each of you? (Stop yelling as much? Feel more in control of your own emotions? Accept not being able to solve every problem? Be OK with your child's negative emotions and be able to stay calm and present with them through the struggles?)

_____

_____

_____

_____

_____

_____

Finally, what support would you need to be able to make those changes? (*Find someone to talk to about your stress level? Become more aware of what triggers your own temper? More sleep?*)

_____

_____

_____

_____

_____

_____

_____

For many parents this will be the first time they've actually thought about how their *own* reaction to a tantrum is either calming a stressful situation, or adding fuel to the fire by enraging their child's downstairs brain. This leads directly to the next Whole-Brain Strategy.

Whole-Brain Strategy #3: Engage Don't Enrage

You'll recall that in the Whole-Brain Child we talked about the importance of engaging your child's upstairs brain as opposed to enraging her downstairs brain. Understanding this strategy offers you an opportunity to avoid a meltdown and teach her skills like compromise, communication, and good decision-making.

The key is to consciously decide which part of your child's brain you want to appeal to when she's having a hard time. If you respond to the off – track behavior with connection first (remember connect and redirect?), and show your child some compassion and understanding, she then feels supported, her defenses begin to settle down, and she is more able to problem solve with you. When you ask your child to think things through, or brainstorm a solution, you are engaging her upstairs brain and helping her return to a state of integration. Keep in mind that if she's really falling apart, her thinking brain won't be working very well and she might need you to help calm her first.

STRATEGY #3

INSTEAD OF ENRAGING THE DOWNSTAIRS BRAIN...

...ENGAGE THE UPSTAIRS BRAIN

WHAT CAUSES A MELTDOWN FOR YOUR KIDS?

Let's give some thought to what causes our kids to flip their lids in the first place. Once we have a clear picture of that, we can make plans to better set them up for success.

What circumstances typically cause your child to melt down? Are there internal triggers, like hunger, a lack of sleep, or illness? Are there particular people who make your child stressed? Loud Uncle Bill? Grandma Sophie with the wet kisses who squeezes way too hard? Maybe the strict science teacher? Or maybe certain events set your child off, like the end of a play date, Mom and Dad going out for date night, or homework deadlines.

In the following chart, fill the left column in with as many examples of these triggers as you can think of. You may even be able to boil some of them down to common triggers such as separation anxiety, difficulty with transitions, or testing boundaries.

Once you've done that, in the right hand column write about how you can be proactive and address these issues so your child's downstairs brain is less likely to become enraged. What clues do you want to look out for? What kind of help would you need to make changes for your kids? We've started off with an example of a typical situation.

Child's Triggers	Possible Solutions
Family gatherings. She's grouchy when we're at my in-laws' house. She never wants the food that's served, she's rude to older family members and doesn't want to hug or kiss them, she always wants to leave early.	1. Have gatherings at our house so she has her own room to recharge in. 2. Come up with a way to greet relatives that feels comfortable for her. 3. Eat before we go/bring her snacks. 4. Problem solve ahead of time about what she can do to entertain herself while there (bring a friend? Bring books/toys/music).

Child's Triggers	Possible Solutions

We're not suggesting that our children should run our lives and that every situation has to be tailored to their likes and dislikes. But you do need to know your own child. In our example, it's possible that the daughter is sensitive to noise and crowds, or is a quiet introvert in a family of loud extroverts. Perhaps it's just that a long family gathering, with nothing age-appropriate for a child to play with or do, is too much to ask at this point. Regardless, you have a choice to make – you can come up with some ways to make the situation easier on your child (and easier on you as well), or you can insist that your child just deal with things as they are, where no one is happy with the situation.

Of course, as we've said before, if you aren't feeling regulated yourself, how can you help your kids? So, let's focus on you for a minute.

What triggers your own downstairs brain?

Think for a minute about what typically sets you off. Is it running late? Feeling judged? Juggling too many responsibilities? What can you do for yourself so that your upstairs brain remains more in control when you're interacting with your kids? Does it have to do with eating better? Sleeping more? Finding time for yourself? Consider these questions below.

Parent's Triggers	Possible Solutions
The morning struggle to get out of the house. I always end up frustrated, stressed, and nagging the kids!	*1. Prepare as much as possible the night before. 2. Start the day better by waking earlier to meditate for 10 minutes. 3. Give the kids more responsibilities. 4. Make a chart of the morning routine for the kids so I don't have to remind them of everything.*

Most of the time people don't think about what triggers them. They just know they get upset! In fact, we're so often unaware that we're being stressed – some of us until we're at the point of explosion – that we *react* from our downstairs brain instead of *responding* from an integrated upstairs brain to what we, or our kids, specifically need. Becoming more aware of triggers and taking steps to reduce them helps us, and our children, keep our brains and bodies in a state of integration.

APPEALING TO THE UPSTAIRS BRAIN

The more opportunities we give our kids to exercise their upstairs brains, the easier it becomes for them to access it when they are losing control of their emotions. Our initial instinct may be to solve problems for our children, or give them the answers when they're struggling, but it's actually when we press our children to do the work themselves that they build the brain muscles they need to develop skills like empathy, self-control, morality, and good decision making.

STRATEGY #4
INSTEAD OF JUST GIVING THE ANSWER...

...EXERCISE THE UPSTAIRS BRAIN

Think about how our own actions can give our kids practice in the sort of behaviors we want them to have. In the left hand column list a few of your child's behaviors, both positive and negative. In the middle column list your own responses that often lead to power struggles, disconnection, or tantrums. Then in the right hand column fill in ways you can appeal to your child's higher thinking and her upstairs brain. Negotiating with her, listening to her feelings, considering alternatives, and compromising are all actions that could fit in this column. Read through our examples, and then come up with your own.

Child's Behaviors	Parent's Action Enrages Downstairs Brain	Parent's Action That Can Strengthen Upstairs Brain
Whining about what's for dinner.	Triggered by whining, your response is to shut down the behavior: *"You get what you get and you don't get upset."*	Acknowledge child's feelings, then negotiate: *"You're upset that we have chicken for dinner tonight, huh? I'm sorry. Can we put our heads together and make a plan for tomorrow that we can both be happy with?"*
Coming out of bedroom, multiple times, after lights out.	Giving in at first, then getting angry that this didn't work: *"I already got you water, tucked you in again and rubbed your back! Why can't you just go to sleep already? It's bedtime!"*	Compassion first, then digging for answers while setting a boundary: *"It seems like something is making it hard for you to sleep tonight. Do you know what it is? How about you tell me about it while I walk you back to bed. It's late and time for you to rest."*
Letting sister borrow favorite shirt.	Ignoring the positive gesture by focusing on what she did wrong: *"That shirt is really expensive! If she ruins it I won't get you another one!"*	Compassion first, then support thinking through her actions: *"That was really generous of you — you made her very happy. How do you think you'll feel if she gets something on it?"*

You've probably found that being compassionate with your child is much easier when your own downstairs brain isn't enraged! Of course, when life is quiet and we don't feel stressed, remaining cool, calm, and connected can be pretty easy. But, just like your kids, when your brain gets overloaded you're more likely to flip your lid!

STAYING ENGAGED

Our days as parents are so busy that taking care of ourselves is often last on the list. However, engaging your own upstairs brain is something simple you can practice each day that can have a significant effect on your relationship with your kids!

When your downstairs brain is enraged, what do you do to engage *your* upstairs brain? What sort of tools do you have that make you pause, reflect, and think before you act?

Here's an exercise that we use sometimes in our workshops:

> *Every night before you go to sleep this week, when you're at your most calm and relaxed, put your hand on your chest. Spend a few seconds noticing how peaceful you feel, free of anxiety or stress.*
>
> *Do that night after night.*
>
> *Then, the next time you feel yourself becoming upset with your kids, return to that pose. You don't even have to lie down. Just put your hand on your chest, take a deep breath, and then exhale. Notice how quickly it can help you calm down and control your emotions.*
>
> *The reason has to do with the fact that neurons that fire together, wire together. Your body is associating this pose with calm and serenity, which means you can return to that pose whenever you want and activate that relaxed state of mind and soothe your whole nervous system.*
>
> *Take a few seconds and try that now. Put your hand on your chest, close your eyes, and let go of everything except this moment. Slowly breathe in and out, and get the feel of what it's like to release your anxiety and tension. Now practice this every night, and use it whenever you feel your downstairs brain beginning to take control.*

This is a really effective method for bringing your brain back to a state of integration. You probably have other tools you've used or have ones that you've heard about that you think may help. Think for a few minutes about what would help you engage your upstairs brain in the heat of the moment. It might be counting to ten, naming three things you love about your child, giving words to your emotions, or some other strategy. Make a short list here of some methods you could try:

_____

_____

_____

_____

Choose one or two ideas from this list (or our method) and make a promise to yourself to practice using them – starting today. New skills take time to build into habits, so give yourself as many opportunities as you can to try these ideas.

Whole-Brain Strategy #4:
Use It or Lose It

Because the functions of the upstairs brain encompass many of the behaviors needed for a successful life, we want to be intentional about making sure we develop this part of our child's brain well. So, not only is it helpful to appeal to our kids' upstairs brains when they're having a difficult time, but we also have to make a point of helping them find ways to exercise this area of their brain on a regular basis.

At the beginning of this chapter we gave you a quick summary of the functions of the upstairs brain. (If you need, return to the section of *The Whole-Brain Child* where we discuss them in detail). Think now about how you can help develop these skills in your child. In the chart below we've given one action step for each goal. Read our examples, and then see if you can come up with two other steps you can take for each.

Goal	Action Step	Action Step	Action Step
Sound Decision-Making	*I'm going to let my toddler have more say in everyday decisions—like picking out her clothes and choosing activities (within reason!)*		
Control of Body and Emotions	*I'm going to model for my child how emotions affect our bodies by talking about how I feel & how I notice it in my own body.*		
Self-understanding	*I'm going to start a parent/child journal that we pass back and forth to each other – we can ask questions, share wishes, explain feelings, and more.*		
Empathy	*I'll add, "What was your act of kindness today?" to our high point and low point of the day dinner ritual.*		
Morality	*At our family meals we will pick a subject – maybe a current event, a sports figure, a newspaper headline, etc. – and encourage discussion.*		

THE WHOLE-BRAIN CHILD WORKBOOK • 51

The brain is like a muscle. Skills like empathy or decision-making take practice to make the muscle strong. The more practice you give your child, the more she'll be able to respond in responsible, respectful, and thoughtful ways.

Of course, this practice applies to *our* brains as well!

DO AS I DO

We always want to keep in mind what we're modeling for our kids with our own behavior. As we teach them about honesty, generosity, kindness, and respect, we want to make sure that they see us living a life that embodies those values as well. The examples we set, for good and for bad, will significantly impact the way a child's upstairs brain develops.

So think about the functions of the upstairs brain as they relate to your own life, and what your kids see you doing. Think about your own decision-making, how well you control your emotions and body, how much you work towards self-understanding, empathy, and morality. In the space below, make a list of ways you set a good example for your kids in these areas, and other areas it would be good for them to see you improve.

_____

_____

_____

_____

_____

_____

_____

If there are areas where you feel there is improvement to be made, make a commitment to begin making those changes. Make notes here about what you need to do, who can help support you, and what steps you will take to begin. Listing action steps engages your upstairs brain!

_____

_____

_____

_____

_____

_____

_____

Intentionally considering your own actions can be a powerful tool. Writing out what's going well, and seeing, in black and white, that improvements have been made, is a great way to calm the emotional and physical stress you may feel at times.

Whole-Brain Strategy #5:
Move It Or Lose It

Research has proven that by the time we consciously realize we are stressed, our bodies already know it. Tension in our shoulders, butterflies in our stomach, and a racing heart are all ways our body sends physical messages to our brain that we're feeling stress. The same goes for our children.

By encouraging your child to change her physical state – either through movement or relaxation – her body will release some of its tension and be able to send calmer information to her upstairs brain. Once this happens, her body and brain are better able to return to a state of integration.

Of course, our kids aren't the only ones who can use this movement strategy. "Move It or Lose It" is perfect for parents to use themselves when they feel overwhelmed or stressed. Here's how we described it in the "Integrating Ourselves" section at the end of Chapter 3 in *The Whole-Brain Child*.

"Move It or Lose It" for parents:
A three-step process

We all have our downstairs moments, when we "lose it" and say and do things we wish we hadn't. In high-stress parenting situations, parents make mistakes. All of us do.

But don't forget: Parenting crises are openings for growth and integration. You can use the moments when you feel yourself beginning to lose control as opportunities to model self-regulation. Little eyes are watching to see how *you* calm *yourself down.* Your actions set an example of how to "make a good choice" in a high-emotion moment when you're in danger of flipping *your* lid.

So what do you do when you recognize that your downstairs brain has taken over and you've begun to lose your mind?

First, do no harm.
Close your mouth to avoid saying something you'll regret. Put your hands behind your back to avoid any kind of rough physical contact. When you're in a downstairs moment, protect your child at all cost.

Second, remove yourself from the situation and calm down.
There's nothing wrong with taking a breather, especially when it means protecting your child. Then, although it might feel a bit silly at times, try out the "Move It or Lose It" technique. Do jumping jacks. Try some yoga stretches. Take slow, deep breaths. Do whatever it takes to regain some of the control you lost when your amygdala hijacked your upstairs brain. You'll not only move into a more integrated state yourself, but you'll also model for your kids some quick self-regulation tricks they can use.

Finally, repair.
Quickly. Reconnect with your child as soon as you are calm, and deal with whatever emotional and relational harm has been done. This may involve your expressing forgiveness, but it may also require that you apologize and accept responsibility for your own actions. This step needs to occur as quickly as possible. The sooner you repair the connection between yourself and your child, the sooner you can both regain your emotional balance and get back to enjoying your relationship together.

Fake it 'til you make it

The "Move It or Lose It" strategy can also be remarkably powerful when our kids are upset. For example, if your preschooler is afraid about an upcoming visit to the dentist or her first piano lesson, you can say something like, *"Show me what your face and body look like when you're brave."* Just acting brave can create those actual emotions in a person, as you and your child will discover.

Or, if your nine-year-old is having a hard time calming down after an altercation with his brother, or feeling especially tense about an upcoming test at school, you can say, *"Pretend that you're a heavy, wet, floppy noodle. What would your body be like?"* Then have him act it out, on the floor or the couch or wherever. The mind-body connection will take over, and the changed posture will result in changed emotions as well.

Sound too good to be true? Try it yourself right now. Act out the following poses, and see how it affects your emotions and mood:

- Brave pose

- Noodle

- Angry face and body

- Huge smile with excitement on face

What did you notice about after doing this exercise? Did your mood change? Is there a difference in how your body feels? How about your emotional state? Detail your experience here:

_____

_____

_____

_____

_____

_____

_____

The more of these exercises you commit to doing, the easier it becomes to model new behavior for your children. And the more we learn about how our brains affect our daily interactions, the more we can pass that knowledge on to our children.

WHOLE-BRAIN KIDS

When children have an understanding of how their brains work, conversations with them about their behaviors and emotions tend to feel much less like personal attacks and more like collaborative problem solving. The upstairs/downstairs brain information is pretty easy for children to understand, and this illustration from *The Whole-Brain Child* is a great way to get that conversation started.

WHOLE BRAIN KIDS: Teach Your Kids about their Downdstairs and Upstairs brain.

YOUR DOWNSTAIRS BRAIN AND YOUR UPSTAIRS BRAIN

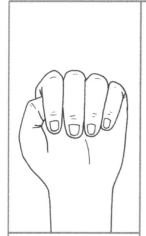

MAKE A FIST WITH YOUR HAND. THIS IS WHAT WE CALL A HAND MODEL OF YOUR BRAIN. RE-MEMBER HOW YOU HAVE A LEFT SIDE AND A RIGHT SIDE OF YOUR BRAIN? WELL YOU ALSO HAVE AN UPSTAIRS AND A DOWN-STAIRS PART OF YOUR BRAIN.

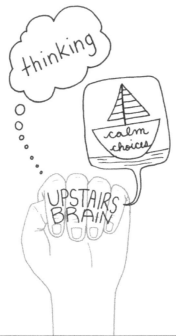

THE UPSTAIRS BRAIN IS WHERE YOU MAKE GOOD DECISIONS AND DO THE RIGHT THING, EVEN WHEN YOU ARE FEELING REALLY UPSET.

NOW LIFT YOUR FINGERS A LITTLE BIT. SEE WHERE YOUR THUMB IS? THAT'S PART OF YOUR DOWN-STAIRS BRAIN, AND IT'S WHERE YOUR REALLY BIG FEELINGS COME FROM. IT LETS YOU CARE ABOUT OTHER PEOPLE AND FEEL LOVE. IT ALSO LETS YOU FEEL UPSET, LIKE WHEN YOU'RE MAD OR FRUSTRAT-ED.

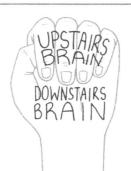

THERE'S NOTHING WRONG WITH FEELING UPSET. THAT'S NORMAL, ESPECIALLY WHEN YOUR UPSTAIRS BRAIN HELPS YOU CALM DOWN. FOR EXAMPLE, CLOSE YOUR FINGERS AGAIN. SEE HOW THE UPSTAIRS, THINKING PART OF YOUR BRAIN IS TOUCHING YOUR THUMB, SO IT CAN HELP YOUR DOWNSTAIRS BRAIN EXPRESS YOUR FEELINGS CALMLY?

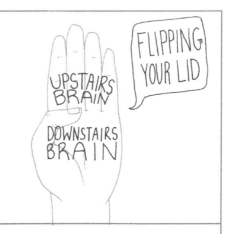

SOMETIMES WHEN WE GET REALLY UPSET, WE CAN FLIP OUR LID. RAISE YOUR FINGERS, LIKE THIS. SEE HOW YOUR UPSTAIRS BRAIN IS NO LONGER TOUCHING YOUR DOWNSTAIRS BRAIN? THAT MEANS IT CAN'T HELP IT STAY CALM.

FOR EXAMPLE:

THIS IS WHAT HAPPENED TO JEFFREY WHEN HIS SISTER DESTROYED HIS LEGO TOWER. HE FLIPPED HIS LID AND WANTED TO SCREAM AT HER.

BUT JEFFREY'S PARENTS HAD TAUGHT HIM ABOUT FLIPPING HIS LID, AND HOW HIS UPSTAIRS BRAIN COULD HUG HIS DOWN-STAIRS BRAIN AND HELP HIM CALM DOWN. HE WAS STILL ANGRY, BUT INSTEAD OF SHOUTING AT HIS SISTER, HE WAS ABLE TO TELL HER HE WAS ANGRY AND ASK HIS PARENTS TO CARRY HER OUT OF HIS ROOM.

SO THE NEXT TIME YOU FEEL YOURSELF STARTING TO FLIP YOUR LID, MAKE A BRAIN MODEL WITH YOUR HAND. (REMEMBER IT'S A BRAIN MODEL, NOT AN ANGRY FIST!) PUT YOUR FINGERS STRAIGHT UP, THEN SLOWLY LOWER THEM SO THAT THEY'RE HUGGING YOUR THUMB. THIS WILL BE YOUR REMINDER TO USE YOUR UPSTAIRS BRAIN TO HELP YOU CALM THOSE BIG FEELINGS IN THE DOWN-STAIRS BRAIN.

After reading the explanation through with your child, you can talk with her to help increase her understanding of how the upstairs and downstairs brains affect the things we all do and the way we all think. Here are some examples of questions that may open the door to a longer dialogue:

- *Have you ever had that feeling where you know what you should do, but you're so upset that you just can't make your body agree to do it?*

- *Remember the other night when I got so angry with you and I yelled? Part of that was my downstairs brain bullying my upstairs brain and taking over! When I was able to calm down, I felt so sorry and I apologized to you. Does that sort of brain bullying ever happen to you or your friends?*

- *What kinds of things make you flip your lid the most? What about your sister – what do you think makes her flip her lid?*

- *When I'm upset and Daddy really listens to me, it helps my downstairs brain calm down. But if he starts getting mad and doesn't listen very well…boy, does that make my downstairs brain mad! Are there things Daddy and I do with you when you're sad or mad that make your downstairs brain get really angry?*

Take a minute now and, using these conversation starters as examples, think about a recent interaction with your child when one of you seemed to have allowed your downstairs brain to take over. Write about that interaction, and then look at it from the perspective of what you know about the upstairs and downstairs brain. What points would be helpful to discuss with your child now?

_____

_____

_____

_____

_____

_____

Having this sort of open dialogue with your children about times they (and you) have felt out of control can be very reassuring to them. It allows them to see that these behaviors occur, that they are still loved, and that their parents are there to support them in learning better ways to handle themselves.

A VISION OF YOUR HOUSE – HELPING CHILDREN UNDERSTAND

Talking about the brain with your children can start early on – the hand model of the brain is great to use even with children as young as three years old! By the time your kids are 5 or 6, the following project is one they should really enjoy doing with you. In fact, doing this alongside them is a great way to model self-understanding.

What you will need: This is essentially up to you, but some suggestions include old magazines, crayons, paint, pens, scissors, glue, paper, any decorative items like glitter, stickers, pom poms, etc.

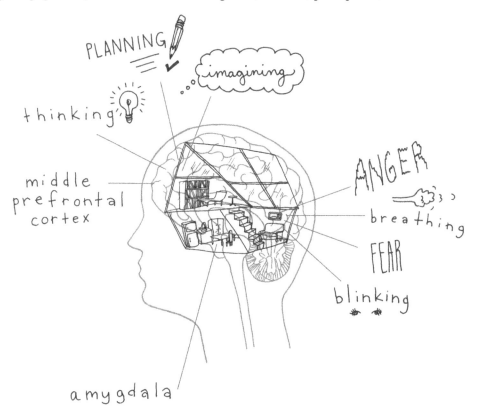

Using the hand model of the brain along with this illustration from *The Whole-Brain Child*, remind your children about the various areas of the brain, their basic functions, and how everyone has an upstairs and downstairs brain. Then ask your children to draw the inside of their "brain/house" with two floors and a connecting stairway. Using magazine cutouts, stickers, or their own drawings, fill the downstairs with words and pictures that describe their downstairs brain and what it may be filled with when it is not operating in connection with the upstairs.

The floor might include the following:

- Colors that embody big emotions (*red anger, blue fear, grey sadness…*)

- Animals or people that express your child's feelings when she feels out of control
  (*scared puppy, roaring lion, crying baby*)

- What their bodies feel like when they are trapped in their downstairs brain
  (*exploding like a volcano, balled up like a hedgehog…*)

- Memories of things they didn't like and how those things felt
  (*a trip to the doctor that made her feel anxious, the day he fell off his bike
  and was scared…*)

Once the downstairs is finished, ask your children to think about the upstairs. Have them put anything there that would help them if the stairway were blocked and they felt stuck downstairs. Ask questions like "What would help calm you down when you feel angry?" or "What makes you feel safe when you're scared?" or "What sorts of things does your body need when it feels uncomfortable or stuck?"

They may come up with ideas such as:

- Pictures of mommy, a warm bath, or a favorite stuffed animal

- Comforting words like hugs, love or kisses

- The memory of a favorite place like the beach or grandma's house

- Exercise, meditating, or a calm-down jar.

This process of creating a visual representation of their brain helps your children integrate their *actual* upstairs and downstairs brains. Your kids are exercising their rational (upstairs) brain as they create, talk, and think about which pictures go where and what they need to help themselves feel better. It also helps them become more aware of their more reactive (downstairs) brain as they recall the feelings associated with the act of losing control and calming down.

When they've finished this project, the picture they will have created can become a vision board to hang in their room. Having it visible gives you (and them) something tangible to refer back to when they become dysregulated or are flipping their lids – a perfect way to engage the upstairs brain when tantrums occur!

Kill the Butterflies
Integrating Memory for Growth and Healing

*Sometimes parents hope their children will just forget about
painful experiences, but what kids really need is for parents
to teach them healthy ways to integrate implicit and explicit
memories, turning even painful memories into sources of power
and self-understanding.*

– The Whole-Brain Child

Generally when we talk about memory, most of us are referring to explicit memories – memories we are aware of – like the time your daughter took her first steps, the vacation you took last summer, or the day your son fell out of a tree and broke his arm.

In Chapter 4 of *The Whole-Brain Child*, we discuss the fact that we also have memories we *aren't* aware of. Even if we can't explicitly recall these memories, they can have a great effect on our lives. In fact, these implicit memories help shape the way we feel about ourselves, about others, and about the world as a whole. It could be argued that certain implicit memories may have an even *greater* effect on our lives than explicit ones, because *we often don't have a sense of recall* when we retrieve them and therefore can't make sense of them – and yet they shade and color our emotions, our behaviors, our perceptions, and even sensations in our bodies. In other words, these implicit memories can shape how we feel and think in the moment even if we aren't aware that these influences from the past are shaping us in the present.

If your child has had difficult experiences in the past, the way memory can work is that the upsetting event can be primarily in implicit memory. The good news is that you can help make the implicit explicit by talking through these memories with your child. In doing so, you shine the light of awareness on feelings, behaviors, thoughts, and bodily reactivity, so they can begin to be understood and explored. If something really painful or scary has occurred in your life or the life of your child, seeing a therapist can be a helpful way to work through traumatic memories. But in many cases, we as parents can offer our kids an enormous gift simply by helping them make their implicit memories more explicit.

Let's start with a quick review of the differences between explicit and implicit memory, and some examples of how they show up in our lives:

Explicit Memory	Examples
Recall of specific memory—either factual or autobiographical which has a feeling of oneself at a point in time	• *"Last week I watched her walk three steps before she lost her balance and fell down!"* • *"Last night I rushed him to the hospital, but his mom was stuck in traffic and it took her a long time to get there."*
Conscious recollection of a past experience with the feeling that the memory is coming from the past	• *"My favorite part of our vacation was when we went blueberry picking."* • *"The kids got along so well on that trip – even when we were stuck inside because of the rain."*

Although we're not aware we are being shaped by them, implicit memories work together with your explicit memories every day. Our implicit memories often map our current reality:

Implicit Memory	Examples
Creates mental models or expectations about the world based on what has gone on in the past—shaping how we feel, how we think, what we believe, and even how we perceive things right now.	• *It's safe for me to cry when I'm hurt.* • *Saying please and thank you to people means they are nice to me and I feel good.* • *I will be comforted when I am upset.* • *We eat popcorn when we watch movies!*
Allows us to automate responses, or respond rapidly, in moments of danger (or perceived danger) without having to actively recall similar instances.	• *I stop and look before I cross the street.* • *I check to make sure the water isn't hot before I wash my hands.* • *I go downstairs feet first.*
Encodes perceptions, emotions, sensations, and, ultimately, behaviors we do "without thinking."	• *I feel excited when Grandpa visits!* • *Dogs are scary! When I see them my heart beats fast and my muscles tense up.* • *I know how to ride my bike.* • *I'm good at math.*

It takes some effort on our part to be aware of what our children may be taking in from their experiences and to help them sort out their thoughts, feelings, and emotions. But by having a working understanding of implicit and explicit memory, we can provide them with what they need in order to develop the resiliency, understanding, and maturity to handle many challenging aspects of life's experiences and to overcome automatic responses when they are problematic.

WHAT IMPLICIT MEMORIES MIGHT BE AFFECTING YOUR CHILD?

All children have moments when they act in ways that seem irrational or unreasonable. However, if you notice behavior that's out of the ordinary – or more extreme than usual – for *your* child, it's possible that an implicit memory is active in shaping her here-and-now experience and perhaps has created a mental model that she needs your help working through.

In the last chapter we asked you to think about what sets your child off and makes her flip her lid. Now let's ask a similar question about memories she might be experiencing. What you are looking for here are *patterns* of behavior where one particular event (*sleepovers, swimming lessons, knives...*) causes problems. Unexplained refusals or avoidance, regressions, fears, or unexpectedly strong reactions can all be signs that there may be some implicit memories that may be impacting your child's response.

In the graphic below, we've used a real experience that happened to Olivia, the 6-year-old daughter of one of our clients. The shaded boxes indicate either non-consciously held emotions and beliefs or stored implicit memories; the white boxes show the child's explicit memory and encoded thoughts:

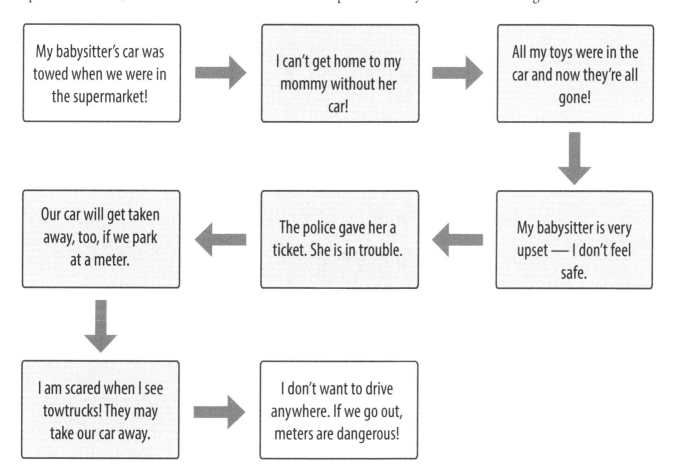

As you can see, there were numerous thoughts that were encoded for Olivia, but all she was really aware of was her fear of parking meters and that she wanted her grown-ups to avoid them. Thankfully her mother was familiar with the reality of non-conscious emotional processes and of implicit memory and was able to talk through the steps of that traumatic event, bringing to light the thoughts her daughter had. With time and patience, this ultimately allowed Olivia to see that it wasn't actually parking meters she was afraid of, and that although the whole experience had been quite frightening for her, it was in the past and there were ways she could understand and have some control over her worries.

Are there non-conscious beliefs and implicit memories that might be affecting your child? Have you noticed times your child's behavior has seemed particularly unreasonable, more intense or irrational than usual? When you look back on these moments, are there any patterns, or any behaviors that strike you as possibly having implicit memories as a contributing factor? For example, does your child have a pattern of overreacting to certain things (*being dropped off at school, learning new skills, particular sounds…*)? Are there experiences he once enjoyed that suddenly he seems not to (*going to the beach, riding his bike, going to bed at night…*)?

When your child is exhibiting difficult behavior, uncovering implicit memories most likely isn't going to be your first response. More likely you'll remember to **HALT** and check the usual suspects first (is your child **H**ungry, **A**ngry, **L**onely, or **T**ired?), then help him by responding to those needs if he has them.

IS YOUR CHILD TOO:

HUNGRY?

ANGRY?

LONELY?

TIRED?

However, helping our children make sense of *past* experiences helps them make sense of their *present*. It allows them to have some sense of control and understanding about what they think, how they feel, and why they behave the way they do.

Give some thought to any extreme behaviors your child may be exhibiting and write them down here:

_____

_____

_____

_____

_____

_____

_____

Now sit quietly for a couple of minutes. As you sit still, see if any thoughts come up for you that might explain your child's behavior patterns. Write down all possible ideas you have about what may be behind his behavior patterns. Think back to conversations you two have had, questions he's asked, or events, large or small, that have occurred prior to any behavior changes that might be related in some, perhaps indirect, way. In looking back with this new level of knowledge, does anything stand out for you? Here's an example to give you an idea of what we mean:

> *Our daughter has been really angry with me lately. I couldn't understand why. Then a possibility occurred to me. I thought it might be because I was in the hospital for a week recently and she didn't see me for so long. Now that I think about it, I am remembering that the first night, my wife stayed overnight with me. When my daughter woke up in the morning, she was scared because Grandma was there instead of Mommy. Then my wife had to spend time away from her, taking care of me while I got better. I wonder if all of this gave her the feeling that I was to blame for that — that I took Mommy away from her.*

We're not suggesting that you impose readings on a situation that might not be accurate, but it's possible that there are times your child may need to return to a difficult moment from the past and could use your help thinking it through. Now that you've read our example, write down any explanations for your child's behaviors that may make sense to you in your own situation:

_____

_____

_____

_____

_____

_____

By talking through these events and helping your child see how her implicit memories may have incorrectly formed a belief system, it's possible to help her put an end to a behavior pattern she seems stuck in.

And of course, this applies to us, as well. We'll come back to our kids' memories in a moment, but first let's look at how memories might be affecting you as you parent.

What memories might be affecting you?

Take a minute to think about times when *you* felt especially anxious, angry, or eager to avoid something. When your response seems disproportionate to the incident, it could be that implicit memories are driving how you're actually reacting. Or maybe you're unsure of why you've developed certain habits or triggers. If you don't have a clear-cut answer for why you do what you do, implicit memories may be involved.

We've offered a few examples in the following chart. Once you've looked them over, see if you can think of any examples from your own past experiences that may contribute to your current thoughts or behaviors. Without having the benefit of someone else pointing out connections for you, when doing this reflection it may be easiest to describe a behavior or thought pattern you are aware you currently have, *then fill* in your best guess at events or experiences that may have lead to the implicit memories that link it all together.

Give it your best shot. The more awareness you bring to these long-forgotten events and memories, the more likely they will start to become clear and you can then make them explicit, and you can begin to piece the puzzle together to understand your behaviors, emotions, and sensations so that they won't rule you.

Present Thought/Behavior	Past Event/Experiences	Implicit Memories
I don't feel good about myself or my body. Overly concerned about appearance and food.	As a child, my mother often criticized her own body and weight and talked about how unhappy she was with her figure.	Women should be thin. Fat is bad. Feeling happy is connected to looking good and being thin.
Fear of taking risks in many areas of life. Concerned with removing life's obstacles for my child so she won't have to take risks to succeed.	After an injury, my overly cautious parents tried to keep me from hurting myself again by restricting my play and frequently told me to be careful.	I am a bad judge of risk. I am not capable of taking care of myself. Risk taking is bad, for me and for my kids. It's too dangerous.

Keep in mind that implicit memories naturally also often contribute to positive behaviors and concepts we all have. However, when a behavior is negatively impacting you or your family, it can be helpful to look more closely at any disturbing events that might have left implicit memories that haven't been integrated.

Whole-Brain Strategy #6:
Use the Remote of the Mind

When it comes to our children (or our own childhood memories), it's important to remember that troubling experiences won't always fit into our grown-up idea of what's traumatic. They can be as simple as falling off a bike, getting scared by the loud hand dryers in the public restroom at the store, or being laughed at. What matters is the way your child processes the experience and then copes with it. In other words, what matters most for having a healthy state of mind is integrating memories of upsetting experiences.

One of the most effective ways to integrate your child's experiences is through storytelling. We've already mentioned a few helpful storytelling strategies *(Name It to Tame It, making a picture book, creating a collage…)* that help integrate left and right hemispheres and the upstairs and downstairs brain.

Sometimes, an experience is too upsetting or painful for your child to be ready to talk about in its entirety right away. This is often a great time to introduce the idea of an internal DVD player with a remote control that he can use to fast forward, rewind, and pause the story. This "remote of the mind" allows your child to have some control over revisiting unpleasant memories. Knowing that he's able to skip past a part he's not ready to talk about can help your child feel more comfortable about allowing you to revisit the narrative of events.

STRATEGY #6

INSTEAD OF FAST-FORWARD AND FORGET...

...TRY REWIND AND REMEMBER

Try this strategy for yourself. Think about a difficult moment from your past, considering the sequence of events both before and after that particular experience. Once you have those details clear in your mind, create a timeline of events similar to the one below.

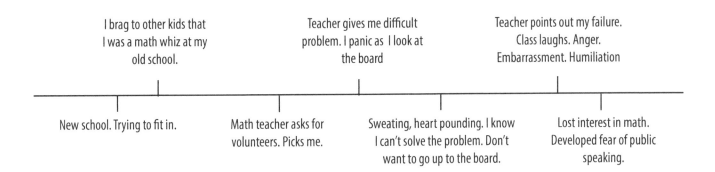

As you can see from this sample experience, there are a number of moments between the initial experience (*being at a new school, trying to fit in*) and the resulting memory (*lost interest in math, developed fear of public speaking*). Because you now know about The Remote of the Mind, you can tell the story of your painful experience but temporarily skip over parts you need to and return to them when you're able to.

At this point create your own timeline in the blank space below. It can look however you want it to. Just fill in all of the detailed memories and then practice telling the story using your remote.

Perhaps there were moments that are too embarrassing to relive right now. Maybe looking at the specifics of what led up to the event causes too much pain when you re-tell the story. That's OK. You can fast forward, rewind, and pause whenever you want to.

HELPING YOUR CHILD TELL A STORY

Revisiting a painful event can be a powerful exercise to try with your child as well. Besides the Remote of the Mind, there are other approaches you can take:

Memory Hopscotch:
Get a large roll of butcher paper to draw out a hopscotch-style time line and have your child hopscotch across his memories, skipping ones he wants to avoid at the moment, landing on ones he feels at ease talking about. Then, as he feels ready, he can hop back and land on ones he skipped until he feels more and more comfortable with all the parts.

Candy Land Recollection:
Create a board game – similar in style to a game like Candy Land – where your child can move her game pieces around the board and choose to skip a memory, go back or forward, stay longer in one spot…whatever she needs.

The beauty of having this control is that you're not changing the details that actually occurred, but *you are choosing when and how you focus on those details.* Having that empowering choice can make the difference between being able to make sense of an experience and hiding from it.

CONNECTING YOUR MEMORIES USING A MEMORY BOARD

Here's another strategy you can use to get more clear on implicit memories. You may recall that in *The Whole-Brain Child* we compared implicit memories to scattered puzzle pieces that the hippocampus helps assemble. We said that we need the light of awareness to shine on implicit memories to make them explicit, thus fitting the pieces together into a recognizable and understandable picture.

We want to give you a chance to do something like that right now: To take the different pieces of a past experience and assemble those pieces into a coherent, recognizable, and understandable picture. You can use this exercise with your kids, but first, try it for yourself. If you don't consider yourself artistic, don't worry. This isn't about doing anything "right." It's about getting clear on our own history, especially one particular experience.

Begin by choosing one of the past experiences you came up with in the earlier reflections—or a different one if you prefer. If possible, pick one that was (or is) especially painful for you – the more emotions you have about the experience, the more you can actually get out of this exercise.

First, gather your supplies:

- A piece of paper that has some weight to it (cardboard, cardstock, poster board, or similar). The larger the paper, the more you can fit on it – so you can determine the size.

- Heavy string, cord, or yarn. It should be thick enough that you can see it when standing a few feet from your creation.

• Glue. Hot glue guns dry the quickest, which makes this project easier, so you may want to pick up one from a crafting store. If not, any type of all-purpose glue will work.

Next, sit quietly and think about the past event you chose. Below, write down anything you can remember from that time (*sensations, images, feelings, thoughts, beliefs, wishes, smells, sounds…*). You may want to include memories from just before the event as well as during and after. Feel free to use additional paper if you need to.

You may be surprised by how many things pop up that feel disconnected – but don't edit yourself! You are trying to get to those implicit memories, the ones that aren't accessed as something coming from the past, and it's possible that what comes to mind within your awareness might not make much sense at first. These may just be images or sensations that on the surface you may not even know why you are putting them down on paper. Just go with your intuition as your rational mind may not be able to say why you've chosen this or that **s**ensation, **i**mage, **f**eeling, or **t**hought. Just **SIFT** your mind, and let arise whatever emerges! Write them down anyway. Later, as you begin to assemble your memory board you can decide what to keep and what will stay.

_____

_____

_____

_____

_____

_____

_____

_____

_____

_____

_____

_____

_____

_____

_____

_____

_____

_____

Now, gather items that symbolize, as much as possible, each of these memories you've sifted out of your mind about the experience you are detailing. Words or pictures cut from magazines are simplest, but if you want to get more creative, you can include things like:

- Pages of a book you were reading during that time

- A scrap of cloth from an old dress you once loved

- A movie ticket stub

- Old photographs

- A pressed flower

- Words that form a quote that makes you think of that time

- Song lyrics

- *Most importantly, find something that symbolizes the specific event you are detailing, and something that symbolizes you—in the present moment.*

Like coming across a long-forgotten toy your child once loved, you may notice that the more specific you get about your memory symbols, the more emotion (and possibly more forgotten memories) will arise within you.

Once you've collected all of your memory reminders, place the symbolic emotional event to the farthest left hand side of the page and the symbol of you in the present moment at the far right side. Keep in mind that some implicit memories will have explicit elements connected to them, so that some parts may feel like they are coming from the past. That's all fine—just go with the experience of assembling these images.

Now use the objects you've gathered to create a timeline of all of your memories. Placement of your memory symbols depends entirely on you. It doesn't need to be a traditional timeline and go in a straight line; it can zigzag and twist if that feels right to you. Many memories may crowd around the event and then, perhaps, there are big, blank stretches of space. Some may circle back around, or overlap. Some may be far apart.

Pay attention to what these memories *feel* like to you, and how you experience them. Do you look back and remember everything in a linear way? Or do your memories get jumbled up at times? Do some feel like they connect directly with others? Do some feel like they make no sense at all? Again, don't edit yet, and *do not glue anything down* until you are happy with the placement of all your pieces. Place everything, then step back to look at it.

You may want to do that several times before you feel like everything "fits" and tells your story. What you're ultimately creating is a representation of your implicit and explicit memories. At the beginning is your painful experience and everything you remember about it. Then, you are intentionally focusing on all of the thoughts, experiences, and emotions you can recall by placing them where they belong between that initial event and the present moment.

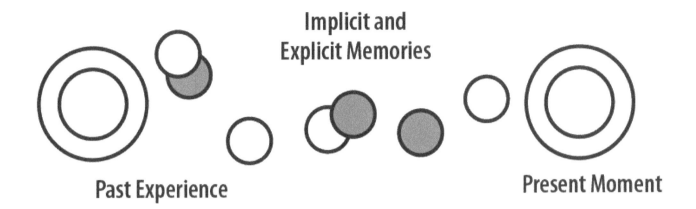

Once all your memories are placed where you want them, glue them down on the board. Next, take your yarn and begin the process of connecting—and integrating—your memories. Glue down one end of the yarn at your past experience. Then run the yarn through your memories, connecting them together – gluing along the way – and eventually connecting them to the symbol of your present day self at the end of the timeline.

Give some thought as you do this to what memories are explicit and connect to each other easily, and which ones may have once been implicit and may be triggering other thoughts. You may decide to use one color yarn for memories that are explicit and clearly connect together, and then another color for ones that were implicit until you began looking more closely. You may want to use many strands of yarn to connect through different memories; maybe old memories that aren't so clear get a different color of yarn, while those that stand out like they happened yesterday get a still different color.

However you decide to create your memory board, and whatever it looks like in the end, what you're doing is taking a symbolic walk through your memory, and examining an experience that was painful to you. If it helps to sort through these as sensations, images, feelings, and thoughts, great! If another way of just letting this all come together works, wonderful! The key is to give yourself the mental space to reflect on these implicit and explicit elements as there is no right or wrong. The very act of making the story is itself an integrative process however it unfolds for you. And doing so can help you gain a clearer sense of how your memories came about, and how they join together to create your present emotions, thoughts, images and sensations. As a result, you'll be integrating implicit and explicit memories and making real sense of a painful experience so that it no longer has the same kind of power over you.

Whole-Brain Strategy #7:
Remember to Remember

Now that you have a sense of how empowering it can feel to really remember details of past events, let's turn our attention to helping your children strengthen their ability to focus on details of the *present* moment.

We know that parents often feel that they have to carve out lots extra time in order to use the parenting tools they learn. But, like all the other strategies we offer in *The Whole-Brain Child*, this strategy focuses on simply being more intentional about using *everyday moments* with our kids helps to help develop their brains and teach them important life and relationship skills. You don't even need yarn or glue!

Remembering to remember goes far beyond asking your child how her day was.

STRATEGY #7
INSTEAD OF "HOW WAS YOUR DAY?"...

TRY "REMEMBER TO REMEMBER"

This strategy is about taking normal, everyday moments, and using them to give kids practice at recollecting important experiences. Asking specific questions, making rituals around remembering details, and creating opportunities to reminisce, are some of the ways we can help our kids get used to focusing on and examining the details of past events. By doing this we help them integrate their implicit and explicit memories – and we parents get the wonderful bonus of being more connected to our kids!

WHAT DO YOU WANT YOUR KIDS TO REMEMBER?

Centuries ago, people knew details of what happened in their lives because stories were told and family history was handed down from generation to generation through songs, books, and conversations. Details got lost or changed over time, but the important stories were ingrained and remembered.

Those of you old enough to remember the days before smart phones and digital cameras may find your early memories a little foggy if your parents didn't engage in a lot of reminiscing with you. But making sure your children do hold on to memories doesn't necessarily require technology.

For this next exercise, come up with a list of important events you want your kids to remember. Start by jotting down ideas that fall into any of the categories in the chart below. We've given you a few ideas to get you started. Add your own memories.

Category	Events
One-Time Family Events	*Family Wedding. The last time we saw Grandma. Graduation. A religious event.*
Traditions	*Family game night. Taco Tuesdays. Camping trips. Decorating the house for the holidays.*
Significant Moments	*Building the tree house together. Raising funds for the animal shelter. Helping the neighbor fix her fence. Our Grand Canyon vacation.*
Miscellaneous Memories	*Learning to make lasagna. Meeting the neighbor with all the cats. The no-hitter we witnessed.*

Our children will have all kinds of memories of past experiences regardless of what we, as parents, do. However, being intentional about remembering is a chance for you to consider ways you can help shape how your children view themselves and your family, how you've spent your time together, and how their view of their past experiences shapes their future.

HELPING YOUR KIDS REMEMBER

Remembering doesn't have to be all about huge, significant, weighty moments. Research shows that kids who engage in "memory talk" have better memories. Memory is a part of the brain's activity, and we want to use remembering to make it stronger, just like a muscle. In addition to the important events you listed above, think also about ways you can help your kids remember when you're going about your everyday life. When you're folding laundry, grocery shopping, or at the doctor's office, what kind of "memory talk" can you do?

You'll recall that we gave you some ideas in *The Whole-Brain Child*, including asking your child to tell you two things that happened today and one that didn't, as well as asking each evening for a high point, a low point, and an act of kindness from the day. Watching old videos and looking at photo albums together are also great ways to help your child recall past events.

Consider your individual, unique kids. What would be most effective in helping them recollect important events you want them to think about? You might have one child who has no trouble talking about what happened during the day. Another child might need a good bit of prompting. Take a few minutes to make a list of intentional ways you can prompt your children to think about their memories. Here are a couple more ideas to get you started:

> *1. Keep a mindfulness journal, writing down moments of each day that you were aware of. Write a few words about your feelings, your surroundings, and anything else you might notice. Share a few of those moments with each other at a family meal, or at bedtime – especially ones where you were with each other. Hearing how different people experience the same event can be eye-opening for children.*

> *2. Ask your kids to draw pictures or write down memories from events, moments, or rituals from everyday life. Put them on small pieces of paper you keep in a "memory jar." These memories can be pulled out (during mealtimes, in the car, while waiting in line...) and revisited together. Kids often love this activity!*

Those are some of our ideas; you can add yours here. How else can you help your family remember to remember?

_____

_____

_____

_____

_____

_____

Helping your children get used to being aware of their daily experiences, teaching them how to look back on past events and remember details, and showing them how their past affects their present are all parts of integrating your kids' memories, helping the implicit become explicit.

WHAT MEMORIES DO YOU WANT TO MAKE WITH YOUR KIDS?

Even as we recollect past experiences, we're constantly creating new traditions and memories as well. We can do so intentionally, setting up rituals and routines that emphasize what's important to us—whether that's family time, helping others, taking care of ourselves as individuals, or whatever else we share as a family.

For example, when Tina's children were very young, she began asking them to write something they were grateful for onto a leaf-shaped paper each year at Thanksgiving. She laminated the leaves and, over time, she created a garland that depicts many of the things they were grateful for and adds to it each year.

The finished collection of what each child was grateful for when they were little, as well as the sight of their childish handwriting from the early days, is sure to bring a rush of memories and emotions – not just for the boys, but for Tina and her husband as well. Meaningful traditions like this one allow a family to share experiences together, and these are the experiences that will likely stand out as memories when children are grown.

Let's give you a chance to think about how you might begin creating new memories and traditions with your family. First, list any routines your family shares that your kids will likely remember in the future. Start with smaller, daily or weekly routines and traditions like your bedtime routine or Friday Family Movie Night. List those here.

_____

_____

_____

_____

_____

_____

Now do the same for less frequent traditions. Maybe a certain summer vacation, or Thanksgiving at Uncle Chris's, or popsicles on the roof on the last day of school.

_____

_____

_____

_____

_____

_____

_____

You may be pleasantly surprised to see that you have more traditions than you thought you did! Now think about others you'd like to set up going forward, and list them here. Think about both daily and weekly events, as well as more seasonal memories you'll create together:

_____

_____

_____

_____

_____

_____

_____

_____

_____

_____

_____

_____

_____

_____

_____

We don't want you to make these ideas anything you'll feel obligated to adhere to rigidly. Just come up with ways to encourage your kids to think about their experiences, and ways to invest your family time with repeated meaning and significance. In addition to bringing your family closer to each other, this type of intentionality helps your children (and yourself) work those memory muscles that ultimately provide them with the ability to make sense of their past experiences.

WHOLE-BRAIN KIDS: TEACH YOUR KIDS ABOUT MAKING THEIR IMPLICIT MEMORIES EXPLICIT

As we've said, one of the best things you can do for a child who is struggling with a past experience is to help her retell the story of what happened. Another reason storytelling is so powerful is that it helps her understand what's happening in her brain when implicit memories of a past experience begin to affect her present thoughts and actions.

WHOLE-BRAIN KIDS: Teach Your Kids About Making Their Implicit Memories Explicit

PUTTING PUZZLE PIECES OF MEMORY TOGETHER

WHEN THINGS HAPPEN, YOUR BRAIN REMEMBERS THEM, BUT NOT ALWAYS AS A WHOLE, PUT-TOGETHER MEMORY. INSTEAD, IT'S AS IF THERE ARE LITTLE PUZZLE PIECES OF WHAT HAPPENED FLOATING AROUND IN YOUR HEAD.

THE WAY YOU HELP YOUR BRAIN PUT THE PUZZLE PIECES TOGETHER IS BY TELLING THE STORY OF WHAT HAPPENED.

TELLING THE STORY IS GREAT WHEN WE DO SOMETHING FUN, LIKE HAVING A BIRTHDAY PARTY. JUST BY TALKING ABOUT IT, WE GET TO REMEMBER HOW MUCH FUN WE HAD.

BUT SOMETIMES, SOMETHING UPSETTING HAPPENS TO US, AND WE MIGHT NOT WANT TO RE-MEMBER. THE PROBLEM IS THAT WHEN WE DON'T THINK ABOUT IT THOSE PUZZLE PIECES NEVER GET PUT TOGETHER, AND WE MIGHT FEEL SCARED, SAD, OR ANGRY WITHOUT KNOWING WHY.

FOR EXAMPLE:

THIS IS WHAT HAPPENED TO MIA. SHE DIDN'T KNOW WHY SHE WAS SCARED OF DOGS. THEN ONE DAY HER DAD TOLD HER A STORY SHE'D FORGOTTEN ABOUT THE TIME A BIG DOG HAD BARKED AT HER.

SHE SAW THAT HER FEARS WERE ABOUT THAT TIME AND NOT ABOUT DOGS SHE MEETS NOW.

NOW SHE LIKES TO PET FRIENDLY DOGS IN HER NEIGHBORHOOD, AND SHE EVENS WANTS A PUPPY OF HER OWN.

WHEN YOU TELL THE STORY ABOUT WHAT HAPPENED, YOU PUT THE PUZZLE PIECES TOGETHER AND YOU FEEL LESS SCARED, SAD, OR ANGRY. YOU WILL ALSO FEEL BRAVER, CALMER, AND HAPPIER.

It really is possible to help a young child see that forgotten explicit or implicit memories of past experiences can be causing current worries. If you want to talk with your child about exploring a past memory, a good way to begin is to read the Whole-Brain Kids illustration together. Then you can continue the conversation however it feels right to you. Here are a few examples of how you might begin:

Do you ever think back to the time you (got separated from us at the grocery store)? Right after that happened, you no longer wanted to (sleep at grandma's house). I know you may not think the two are connected, but it's kind of like those are two sides of a puzzle and the middle pieces are missing! I bet if we fill in the missing pieces we could help you not have that worry anymore. Want to try?

I notice that there are times that something kind of small happens, but your reaction to it is really huge – like how you got so upset when you had trouble remembering those dates for your history test. Did you know that sometimes the reason for that is because you have memories in your brain that you actually don't remember? Those memories can make you get mad or sad or scared about things, but because you don't remember you have those memories, your big feelings just feel like they are coming from nowhere! Isn't that weird?

So, you know how you use Google to search for information? Did you know that there's a part of your brain called the hippocampus that's kind of like a search engine? Whenever you experience something like (helping me cook dinner, meeting new people, getting on an airplane…), your brain does a little search to find memories that match that experience. The thing is, like in this cartoon, if your search engine can find only some of the memories, because the others are hidden, it's not always able to get the right information! So, if the only thing you remember about cooking dinner with me is that one time you burned your hand, you might never want to cook again. But, because we talked about that time a lot, you also remember that you burned your hand because you weren't being very careful, and because you were little back then. So now when your search engine looks for memories about cooking, you know that you're bigger now, and that if you're careful, cooking is a fun experience, not a scary one!

WHOLE-BRAIN KIDS EXERCISE: MAKING A MEMORY BOOK

Talking through unsettling experiences to unlock implicit memories is one way to strengthen your children's ability to feel more in control of their feelings. Helping your kids make more of their memories explicit right from the start is another.

You've heard us talk about making a memory book to help your child retain details about important events that she might otherwise lose over time. This can be a fun project to do with your child while creating some happy, explicit memories. It can also inspire him to create more memory books on his own as he gets older.

Your memory book can be any style at all – from a freeform scrapbook to a formal photo album – whatever appeals to you and your child. After deciding on what experience to focus your memory book on, begin collecting any items that have some symbolic meaning to your child.

For example, if your book is going to be about a recent family vacation, you might include photos, seashells, train schedules, restaurant menus, circus tickets, a map or foreign currency, and the like. As each item goes into the book, have your child write (or dictate) descriptions. He may want to include notes like where he was, who was with him, what he was thinking, how he was feeling, what the weather was like, and so on. By getting used to noticing all of these various parts of his memory of the event, he will not only become more aware of how his experiences affect him, but he'll also begin to retain more detailed memories of these special moments in his life.

This is just one more way to give kids practice remembering and to help them integrate their memory by making the implicit explicit.

CHAPTER 5

The United States of Me
Integrating The Many Parts of Self

> By directing our attention, we can go from being influenced by
> factors within and around us to influencing them. When we
> become aware of the multitude of changing emotions and forces
> at work around us and within us, we can acknowledge them
> and even embrace them as parts of ourselves – but we don't have
> to allow them to bully us or define us.
>
> – The Whole-Brain Child

One of the greatest gifts we can give our children is the ability to understand their own minds, as well as the minds of others. This ability is referred to as "mindsight," a term coined by Dan in his academic text, *The Developing Mind,* and explored in great detail in his popular book *Mindsight.* Mindsight is about seeing and understanding ourselves, as well as seeing and understanding the people in our lives. In this chapter we'll focus on the first half of that equation, understanding our own mind. Then in the next chapter we'll talk about the importance of taking our "me," and joining with others so that we can become a "we."

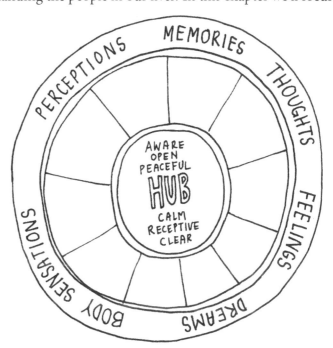

In this chapter we focus on the Wheel of Awareness. To remind you: Your mind can be pictured as a bicycle wheel, with a hub at the center and spokes radiating toward the outer rim. The rim represents anything we can pay attention to or become aware of: our thoughts and feelings, our dreams and desires, our memories, our perceptions of the outside world, our connections to others, and the sensations from our body.

The hub is the inner place of the mind from which we become aware of all that's happening around and within us. The hub is the "knowing" of awareness, whereas the rim is the "known" in all its full spectrum. It is from this hub of awareness that we send out a spoke of attention to focus on the various points on the rim of our wheel.

STUCK ON THE RIM: DISTINGUISHING BETWEEN "FEEL" AND "AM"

If you've ever had the experience of being kept up at night by a thought you can't get out of your head, or found yourself coming back to a worry that keeps you from enjoying whatever else you're doing, or felt so anxious that you had knots in your stomach, then you know what it's like to get stuck on one rim-point on your Wheel of Awareness. This is "getting lost on the rim."

When your child gets "stuck on the rim," most likely she's become overly focused on just a few rim-points (*That Halloween mask was so scary. I'm worried about doing well in math this year. What if I forget my lines in the school play? ...*) and has lost the ability to see the full picture—the full range of other things on the rim. Instead of seeing the world from broad perspective of her hub, she sees only those particular points that create an anxious and critical state of mind, and loses sight of other aspects of her life that can help her feel more balanced and happy.

The hub gives us a flexible and spacious sense of being aware of our lives. Being lost on the rim can make us feel rigid and tightly contained. The idea is to balance our experience of the hub and the rim—to link these two in what is called an "integrated consciousness." While for adults this is a practice you yourself can try at Dan's website (DrDanSiegel.com), and for adolescents you can experience this directly in Dan's book, *Brainstorm,* in *The Whole-Brain Child* we offer this useful view of the mind for children.

Being stuck in a state where kids are aware of only what isn't working can lead them to become confused about the difference between "feel" and "am." It can be hard for a child to understand the difference between saying "I *feel* stupid" and saying "I *am* stupid." This can lead her into simply defining herself by how she feels in the moment. "I *feel* lonely" or "I *feel* like a failure today" can become, instead, "I *am* lonely" or "I *am* a failure." Feelings come and go; but identity expressed as "I am" can feel fixed and unchangeable. In other words, your child's momentary state of mind – her temporary *state* of being – is instead perceived as a permanent *trait* that defines who she is as a person.

STATES, TRAITS, AND YOUR CHILD

Let's start by taking a look at the common complaints you hear from your kids. In the space below, write their complaints about everything from siblings, to their situation, to what they say about themselves (*I'm bored; She's so mean; I hate math; I'm terrible at hockey....*).

_____

_____

_____

_____

_____

_____

_____

Now look at this list. How often do your child's momentary feelings, or states, get expressed as if they were unchangeable characteristics, or traits, describing the totality of their being? Keep this idea in mind as you move through this chapter of the workbook. Later in this chapter, we'll give you a chance – and some directions – about how to explore these ideas with your kids, using their own Wheel of Awareness.

First, though, turn your attention to yourself, considering the same question you considered about your child above: When you talk about your own life, what are your most common complaints? (*My oldest son is so lazy; My kids never pick up after themselves; I'm so tired; I'm feeling sad about what happened at work today; Why do I have to be the parent whose kid is sick all the time?....*). As you're writing, take notice of whether your complaints are phrased as states ("I feel") or traits ("I am") – but don't change them! Write them down as you would normally think or say them.

_____

_____

_____

_____

_____

_____

As you've seen in previous chapters, becoming aware of your own behavior patterns helps you not only understand yourself better, but also model the sort of awareness you want to encourage in your children. Becoming conscious permits choice and change.

YOUR OWN WHEEL OF AWARENESS

Using the list above, let's help you set up your own Wheel of Awareness. You can draw your own to make it look like one of those provided here.

In the conventional version of the wheel practice (aimed at adolescents and adults), you'll notice that the rim is divided into four sections: the first five senses from sight to touch; the internal sensations of the body; mental activities of emotions, thoughts, memories and beliefs; and the sense of connection within relationships to others. The spoke represents attention, and it can be moved around to focus attention from the hub of knowing within awareness to any particular place on the rim of what can be known. This framework can set the stage for how you might explore your own rim-elements, sending a spoke of attention throughout the full range of what is on the rim.

For younger people, just having a wide-open rim may be the most useful approach, offering them the freedom to simply focus that spoke of attention on whatever is most relevant for them in the moment.

Whichever way you choose for yourself, it's not important how neat it looks, as long as it's helping you think about your own thoughts and feelings, and where you focus your attention.

Begin by filling in some rim-points. Take the negative feelings you mentioned above, the ones that really get to you, and write them around the rim of the wheel. But as you do so, add in the positive aspects of your life as well. Little things like *"There was less fighting at breakfast this morning"* or *"I found time today to work on this workbook!"* are just as important to acknowledge as big things, like *"My daughter is becoming so responsible"* or *"My son is starting to calm down on his own when he gets angry."*

After filling your rim with these various points, go back to the thoughts that upset you or drive you crazy. Take a minute to notice how those complaints feel now that they're put into perspective with your life overall.

It's not at all that you should deny your less pleasant feelings and experiences. On the contrary, these are important for you to look at and deal with. But, by seeing your life as a whole, you are less likely to let those negative feelings become your overall perspective. You'll recognize that many of them are temporary states of mind, as opposed to traits that describe who you really are.

THE POWER OF FOCUSED ATTENTION

The point here is to focus on how and where we focus our attention. We can choose to look at positive, upbeat rim-points at any time—not to ignore the more negative rim-points, but to make sure we're balancing ourselves and maintaining a full perspective.

You'll recall that in *The Whole-Brain Child,* we discussed the concept of neuroplasticity, or how the brain physically changes depending on what we experience and what we give our attention to. Remember that neurons that fire together, wire together. In other words, our experiences and thoughts cause our neurons – or brain cells – to activate, which in turn enables new connections to be wired among those neurons that are activated at the same time.

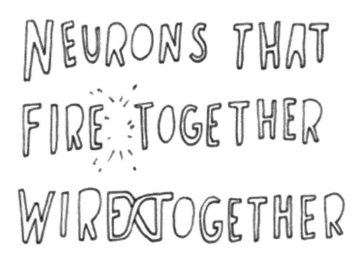

This explains why focusing only on particular aspects of our rim, and not others, can get us stuck dealing with certain emotions and preoccupations. Giving all of our attention to one particular rim point will impact not only our psyche and mood, but our very brain itself. However, by learning to shift that focus, we can also learn to shift our mental state. If each day you do a regular Wheel of Awareness reflective practice (which you can find on Dan's website), you'll learn to develop this capacity to be mindful, to literally strengthen your mind and integrate your brain!

Integrating means the linkage of different parts. And that's what you did above, when you focused on different, more affirming rim-points. You may have been stuck on a rim-point that left you feeling grumpy, because it's the end of a long day and your son refused to take a bath (again), but then you spent a few minutes looking at all the parts of your life and your attention was able to shift to the fact that your daughter is finally out of diapers or that you had lunch today with an old friend.

Write about that experience now. Articulate how things changed for you, emotionally, when you shifted your attention, and anything else you noticed when you filled in your Wheel of Awareness.

_____

_____

_____

_____

_____

_____

_____

_____

_____

_____

We realize that some problems aren't so easy to get past. Sometimes we get "stuck on the rim" and unable to focus on anything except for one unpleasant rim-point (*worrying about a promotion at work, concern over your child's behavior at school, stressed about paying bills…*). We don't mean to be glib, and we're not saying it's always easy to focus on positives when it feels like life is crashing down on us. But the more anxiety and stress you feel when focusing on those problems, the more your brain builds neural pathways that link negative associations with those problems-and the more stress and anxiety become a natural reaction for you.

So even though it's not easy, you'll do yourself a huge favor if you'll simply practice shifting your focus to the more positive rim points on your wheel. Doing this on a regular basis can bc a great practice that enhances your life.   As a result, you'll not only begin to notice happier and more peaceful feelings, but you'll also be strengthening your brain's ability to more automatically shift when stressful thoughts begin.

GETTING BACK TO THE HUB

When you focus your attention and shift your mental and emotional state, you're getting back to the hub of your wheel. Remember, the hub helps create a state of integration where you are experiencing neither chaos nor rigidity, but rather feel the experience of inner harmony. Some describe the hub as an inner sanctuary, a place of peace and clarity. From this calm, peaceful state you can remain aware of all the aspects of your life – both positive *and* negative – without getting stuck on any one point.

The key is to strengthen the hub of your mind so you experience it more frequently and so that you can more readily access this place whenever you need to!

What gets you back to your hub when you feel stressed, anxious, depressed, or otherwise disintegrated? For some, taking time to do an active reflective practice, a form of meditation, can be useful. Rather than doing this only when you're in a tough spot, practicing the Wheel of Awareness on a regular basis can be a great way to strengthen access to the hub of your mind. Other ways people find to reconnect might include physical exercise. For others it's time with – or away from – family. It might be some of the things we've discussed throughout this workbook, like telling your story, integrating your memory, or a combination of more than one of these ideas. Take a couple of minutes now and think about what you do when you need to get back to your hub. What specific, practical steps can you take when you feel yourself out of balance?

_____

_____

_____

_____

_____

_____

_____

_____

_____

_____

_____

_____

_____

_____

_____

Returning to your hub not only results in getting to enjoy a more positive outlook on life, but also in being able to work out difficult situations from a state of open awareness, as opposed to a state of stress.

Whole-Brain Strategy #8:
Let the Clouds of Emotion Roll By

As adults we know that feelings are temporary—they come and they go. We have years of memories that remind us that sometimes we might feel joyful, at other times angry – and those feelings, no matter how big, will eventually change. But our kids don't always know this. They need our help to understand that even overwhelming emotions like fear, frustration, and loneliness are temporary states, not enduring traits.

Keep in mind that even though you want your kids to know that their feelings aren't permanent, that doesn't mean you should be dismissive of their emotions. All feelings – your own, as well as your children's – should be taken seriously and given respect. In doing so, you're showing them that it's OK for all feelings to be felt, while also helping them see that feelings do ultimately change. The more kids can grasp this concept, the less likely they will be to get stuck on the rim of their wheel, and the more likely they are to live life and make decisions from their hub.

STRATEGY #8

INSTEAD OF DISMISS AND DENY...

...TRY TEACHING THAT FEELINGS COME AND GO

LETTING FEELINGS GO: A GUIDED EXERCISE

Here's a mindsight exercise to help you experience first-hand this point about changing emotions:

> *Go back to what you wrote above, when you listed negative emotions you sometimes get stuck on. Choose one of these rim points to think about, then close your eyes and picture the negative emotion as a cloud. Focus on that cloud and notice its details. What size is it? Is it grey and stormy looking? Or maybe it's white and fluffy. Is it clearly defined or wispy and shapeless? What feelings do you get when you see it – does it feel ominous and threatening, or perhaps more low – lying and sad? Don't make judgments about your cloud, or about how you should feel about it. Just notice what you notice. While you sit with those sensations, acknowledge that this cloud is important and real and something to pay attention to – just as all of your emotions are.*
>
> *Like any cloud you see in the sky, your cloud may seem to sit still and linger at times. But if you continue to watch it, you'll notice that it's actually floating along and will eventually drift out of sight. You may notice that you have thoughts in your head as you go through this visualization ("This is weird"; "My cloud is huge – it's never going to move"; "how long do I have to do this?"...). Let these thoughts, just like your cloud, come into your awareness without judgment. Then let them move along out of your consciousness. You'll notice that as they pass, new thoughts come up ("I'm not supposed to judge my cloud!"; "I feel tired"; "Wow, my cloud is getting smaller"...). Again, just let those thoughts come up and move on. Stay with this exercise for one to two minutes, or until you see your cloud disappear as it drifts out of sight.*

Once you open your eyes, write about your experience. What sensations did you notice as your cloud disappeared? Did other emotions take its place? Do you feel a sense of emptiness? Relief? Agitation?

_____

_____

_____

_____

_____

_____

_____

_____

_____

_____

Acknowledge to yourself that this cloud will likely reappear (possibly even right away), but the more you allow it to roll on by each time it pops up, the more you'll see that it's only one of many emotions that will come and go.

A guided meditation like this is a wonderful exercise for children. You'll want to choose a quiet, comfortable place where you won't be disturbed, and keep your voice calm and gentle so your child feels relaxed. If you're offering up images or asking questions, give your child time to consider what you're saying – not so he can give you an answer necessarily, but just so he can connect with your words. You can use the concept we outlined, or follow a script like this:

Close your eyes and take a slow, deep breath…in through your nose…1, 2, 3, 4, 5. Now, blow out through your nose — 1, 2, 3, 4, 5. Fill your lungs again, breathing through your nose…1, 2, 3, 4, 5 and out through your nose…1, 2, 3, 4, 5.

Good. As you continue to breathe deeply, allow your body to relax into your chair (bed, couch…). Now imagine your anxiety (your worry about gym class, your fight with your friend…) as a cloud in the sky.

Look at this cloud closely. Can you see any details? You don't have to tell me if you don't want to…you can just notice whatever you notice. There's no right or wrong answer. Maybe it's a white, fluffy cloud…or maybe you see it as a dark, stormy one. When you look at it, does it seem high and far away, or maybe low and covering most of the sky? Does the look of your cloud make you feel anything in your body? Do you feel those feelings in any particular place? Can you lay your hand where those sensations are?

Sometimes our clouds make us feel sadness, or frustration, or maybe even anger. Whatever you're noticing, just allow yourself to be aware of it all. There's no need to change or judge your thoughts – they're all OK to have. Now bring your attention back to your cloud. I want to remind you that your cloud is real and important, and it's something to pay attention to – just like all of your emotions.

As you sit and watch it float by in the sky, has your cloud changed shape or color? Is it moving quickly or does it seem to be staying in one place? Remember, sometimes clouds look like they're going to sit there forever, but there's always movement – even if we aren't aware of it. As you are taking deep breaths and blowing out, you might imagine that you're blowing your stormy clouds away. With a little time, every cloud moves on and then new clouds – just like new feelings – come into view!

That's what I want you to imagine now – your cloud has moved on from your view and new clouds are gently drifting in. They look and feel different from the one that was just there. There are many of them filling the sky in front of you – some grey and dark, some wispy white ones – and there's plenty of blue sky as well.

That first cloud, with all of the thoughts and feelings it brings, might come back again – it might even come back soon. But you know now that clouds and feelings are similar – they come and they go. No single cloud stays in your sky forever.

Take another deep breath, …1, 2, 3, 4, 5. And breathe slowly out …1, 2, 3, 4, 5. Once more. In …1, 2, 3, 4, 5. And out …1, 2, 3, 4, 5. Bring your attention back to your comfortable spot in the chair (on your bed, on the couch) and slowly open your eyes.

At times, guided meditations can bring up a lot of emotions that haven't been expressed fully, so be prepared to support your child if he has some big feelings during this exercise.

Whole-Brain Strategy #9:
SIFT – What's Going On Inside

This particular strategy, like so much of *The Whole-Brain Child*, is all about awareness. In order for kids to develop mindsight and then influence the different thoughts, desires, and emotions whirling around within them, they first need to become aware of what it is they're actually experiencing. That means one of our most important jobs as parents is to help each of our children recognize and understand the different rim points of their individual wheel of awareness.

You will recall that **SIFT** helps our children pay attention to the **s**ensations, **i**mages, **f**eelings, and **t**houghts that are affecting them. This chart should give you an easy visual reminder of how this strategy breaks down.

SIFT	Description	Example
Sensations	By paying attention to your physical sensations, you become more aware of what's going on in your body.	*Stomach butterflies might mean nervousness. Tightness in your throat could mean sadness. Clenching your jaw may be anger.*
Images	Images can affect the way you look at and interact with the world. Being aware helps you take control and diminish the power the images have over you.	*Images of past experiences (scary, embarrassing, confusing…) and fabricated images (from dreams, movies, books…) can begin to be controlled. See the illustration below.*
Feelings	Developing a rich, descriptive language to talk about the complexity of your emotions allows you to express yourself fully and be deeply understood.	*Help kids go from a vague sense of being "mad" or "sad" to having the descriptive language that allows them to know precisely when they have feelings of being "anxious," "jealous," or "excited." The following chart is especially helpful for young children.*
Thoughts	Learning to pay attention to the thoughts running through your head, and understand that you don't have to believe every one of them. This allows you to direct your attention away from rim points that are limiting, and toward those that lead to happiness and growth.	*What we think about, what we tell ourselves, our beliefs, and how we narrate the story of our own lives, using words. Argue with ideas that aren't helpful or healthy for you. See if you can find a more optimistic perspective on negative self-talk that holds you back.*

FEELINGS

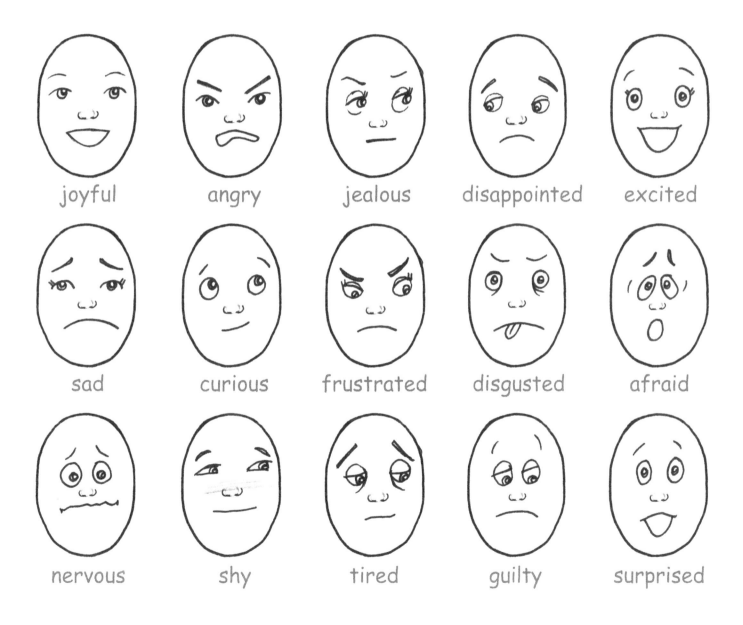

joyful   angry   jealous   disappointed   excited

sad   curious   frustrated   disgusted   afraid

nervous   shy   tired   guilty   surprised

By teaching our kids to SIFT through the activity of their mind, we are showing them how to recognize these different rim points at work within them, and are helping them gain more insight and control in their lives.

A SIFTing exercise

As with anything you want to teach, being able to experience it first makes it easier to convey a deeper understanding to others. So take a minute now and try SIFTing through your own mind. Don't worry about a specific, direct payoff here. This exercise is more about getting in touch with what's going on inside you. Something may come up that you want to think more about or deal with, but the point is simply to notice what's there.

Begin this reflection by finding a quiet place you can sit without interruption. Next, close your eyes and start to bring your attention to whatever bodily sensations you become aware of. You may find it easier to scan your body from head to toe (or in reverse) if there's not a particular sensation that jumps out for you. Write down whatever sensations you noticed (*"My stomach feels tight and jittery"; "My head feels tired and fuzzy"; "I feel relaxed"; "My feet feel heavy"...*) and if those sensations felt connected to anything worth paying attention to (*"My stomach's tightness reminded me that I am upset with my sister", "The tired fuzziness tells me I haven't eaten today"...*). If you like, you can jot down any notes about what you notice:

_____

_____

_____

_____

_____

Next, on to noticing any images that come to you. Again, close your eyes and relax. Do any pictures come to your mind? Perhaps you see images from something that happened earlier in the day, or from your dreams, or maybe even your childhood. Take a minute or two and notice whatever comes up. The images you see may represent both difficult experiences as well as positive ones. Some may disappear quickly, while others refuse to leave. Sometimes images are symbolic and at other times the reference is very direct. The images you see can give you some indication of what you may be struggling with or where your attention is fixed or what's keeping you stuck on your rim. Take a minute to write some notes about what you became aware of:

_____

_____

_____

_____

_____

_____

When you're ready, continue by SIFTing through your feelings and emotions. This can be difficult for some people who aren't used to exploring their feelings and who may be more comfortable with left-brain, logical thinking. Remember, all feelings are acceptable, but for some people this can bring up some discomfort depending on how expressing emotions was handled as you were growing up. Be patient with yourself, and do your best not to judge your feelings as you notice them.

Notice your feelings for as long as you are comfortable doing it; when you're finished, you can make some notes about what you've become aware of:

_____

_____

_____

_____

_____

_____

_____

_____

_____

_____

_____

_____

Finally, focus on your thoughts. Remember, thoughts can be what we think about, what we tell ourselves, our beliefs, and how we narrate the story of our lives. You may find that when you pay focused attention to your thoughts, they lead you to a better understanding of why you react in a certain way or have certain beliefs.

For example, take a look at this flow chart of a thought pattern that came up for one of Tina's adult clients when she did this reflection.

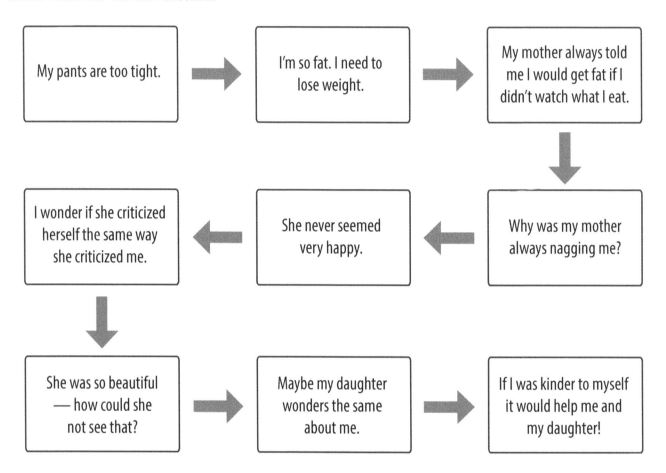

Before learning to pay attention to her train of thought, this woman often got stuck on the rim with the thought *"I'm so fat. I need to lose weight"*. But because she was SIFTing through her thoughts, she was working on just being aware of what thoughts came up for her. This ultimately led her to a realization about herself (and her mother); this awareness allowed her to begin to break free of a negative thought pattern so she could return to her hub

Sometimes thoughts are disconnected and don't lead you to any sort of breakthroughs. That's just fine! Don't pressure yourself to have an epiphany! We just want you to get comfortable with noticing your thoughts and to be aware that you don't have to believe every thought that enters your mind.

In fact, one important skill you can develop as you learn to pay more attention to your thoughts is to argue with the ones that are unhelpful or unhealthy, and direct your attention toward ones that make you happy or push you toward achieving your goals! Here's how it might work for an older child facing a potentially scary process:

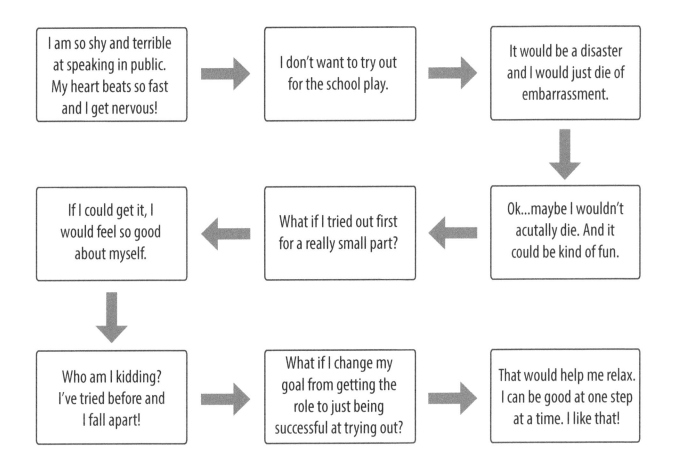

Being able to see that a thought can be argued with – even if it's a thought that you're stuck on – can give you (or your child) an enormous sense of control. Understanding that your thoughts don't have to control you, and that you have a say in how you feel, is an empowering lesson to learn.

With that understanding, take a minute now and sit quietly, and notice what thoughts begin running through your mind. Follow them. Argue with them if you need to, see where they lead, become aware of how you talk to and about yourself and your life. Do this for as long as you're comfortable and then write down what came up for you:

_____

_____

_____

_____

_____

_____

_____

In looking back over this SIFTing exercise, if there were any sensations, images, feelings or thoughts that came up more powerfully for you than others, you might want to investigate them further – possibly by visiting with older relatives who may recall details, talking to a professional therapist, asking for support from a close friend, or something else.

HELPING YOUR KIDS SIFT AND SHIFT

Now that you've personally experienced what SIFTing can accomplish, and how it can help you develop mindsight, think about how that process could be helpful for your kids. By teaching our children to SIFT through the activity of their mind, we can help them recognize the different forces at work within them and help them gain more insight and control in their lives. SIFTing also helps kids understand the important lesson that our bodily sensations shape our emotions, and our emotions shape our thinking, our perceptions, and the images in our mind. *In other words, all of the points on the rim – sensations, images, feelings, and thoughts – can influence the others, and together they create our state of mind.*

Let's get specific by naming issues that face your child, and how you might respond to each situation. What fears or issues cause him trouble? How can you help him develop his own understanding of himself and focus his attention in ways that help him take charge of his emotions and reactions to his world? Consider each of the elements involved in helping your child SIFT so you can help him *shift* his way of looking at those situations he struggles with. We'll start you off with a couple of examples, then you can fill in the rest of the chart with specifics that fit your family.

Issue #1
Separation anxiety at school drop off

SIFT Solutions for Issue #1
SENSATIONS: Arrive at school early enough to find a quiet spot to tune in to the uncomfortable sensations she feels anticipating drop off. Help her imagine each sensation being put into a balloon then ask her to blow the imaginary balloon up using deep breathing (in through the nose, out through the mouth). When the balloon is full, release it – and the uncomfortable sensations – into the air. Afterwards, ask her to connect to how relaxed both her brain and body feel.
IMAGES: During a quiet time with your child, ask her to describe the images that come up when she thinks about being dropped off at school. Help her turn scary images into silly ones or sad images into happy ones by talking through what each image needs in order to shift to its opposite. (See the following illustration.)
FEELINGS: Work with your child to list everything that makes her feel good about school. Together, make a picture book that you can read each morning before drop off. Remind her that her worried feelings about Mommy and Daddy saying goodbye are real, but they are just a very small part of her day. The rest of her school day is what makes up this book. Each time you read the book, her brain builds stronger neural connections to the good feelings she has about school.
THOUGHTS: Teach your child about not having to believe all her thoughts, and have her imagine talking to her brain whenever she hears it making unhelpful comments. Remind her that she can argue with her brain. You can even teach her to name that negative voice inside her. In making this silly, you relieve some of the tension while helping her see that she has control over the situation. When she starts to get upset at being dropped off, bring up that negative voice in a gently joking way: *"Is that Stinky Steve talking again? Stinky Steve doesn't know anything about your school! Stinky Steve, stop telling Lucy that Mommy won't come back – you're always trying to trick her! Lucy, what do you want to tell Stinky Steve?"* Have your child write down (or tell you) all the thoughts she has about being dropped off at school. Put them into two columns – one for helpful thoughts, one for unhelpful thoughts. Then have a conversation with Stinky Steve (or whatever name you give that negative voice).

Issue #2

SIFT Solutions for Issue #2

SENSATIONS:

IMAGES:

FEELINGS:

THOUGHTS:

Issue #3

SIFT Solutions for Issue #3
SENSATIONS:
IMAGES:
FEELINGS:
THOUGHTS:

Because SIFTing integrates your entire system – physical, mental, and emotional – the process of looking at each aspect of how we're affected by events can be really effective at helping your child get unstuck from issues that feel particularly overwhelming.

STRATEGY #9
INSTEAD OF DISMISS AND DENY...

...TRY USING MINDSIGHT TO TAKE CONTROL OF IMAGES

The SIFT Game

Another way to introduce the idea of SIFTing to your child is to turn it into a game. You may remember this one from *The Whole-Brain Child*. The next time you have a few minutes in the car with your kids, start the game by asking questions that aid the SIFTing process.

You: I'll mention something about what the sensations of my body are telling me. I'm hungry. What about you? What's your body saying?

Your child: The seatbelt feels scratchy on my neck.

You: Oh, that's a good one. I'll adjust it in a minute. What about images? What pictures are going through your mind? I'm remembering that hilarious scene from your school play, and you in that funny hat.

Your child: I'm thinking about the preview we saw for that new movie. The one about the aliens?

You: Yeah, we've got to see that. Now feelings. I'm really feeling excited about Grandma and Grandpa coming tomorrow.

Your child: Me, too!

You: OK, S – I – F…. Now "T" for "thoughts." I just thought about how we need milk. We'll need to stop before we get home. What about you?

Your child: I've been thinking that Claire should have to do more chores than me, since she's older.

You: (smiling) I'm glad you're so good at coming up with ideas. We'll have to give that one some more thought.

Even if things get silly, the SIFT game is a good way to give your kids practice at paying attention to their inner landscape. And remember that just by talking about the mind, you help develop it.

Whole-Brain Strategy #10:
Exercising Mindsight: Getting Back to the Hub

When kids become fixated on something they're struggling with (one set of points on their wheel of awareness), we can teach them how to shift their focus, so they can become more integrated. They can then see that they don't have to be *controlled* by their sensations, images, feelings, and thoughts – they get to *decide* how they think and feel about their experiences.

Although this concept may sound appealing and straightforward, it's actually not something that typically comes naturally to children—or even to many adults! However, teaching your kids how to shift their minds to the hub and to focus their attention on a range of points on the rim is something you can help them with. By giving them tools and strategies for calming themselves, and for integrating their different feelings and desires, you're introducing them to mindsight tools that help them become more focused and centered. From this state of open and flexible awareness (their hub), they're able to remain aware of the many varied rim-points affecting their emotions and state of mind. The hub is the beginning of not only clear awareness, but ultimately is the wellspring for wisdom as they mature in later years.

STRATEGY #10
INSTEAD OF DISMISS AND DENY...

...EXERCISE MINDSIGHT

A helpful mindsight tool is a simple reflective practice that can help kids (or their parents!) be more mindful in the present moment. Remember the two exercises we detailed in *The Whole-Brain Child*—the one about breathing, and the one about being underwater, calm as the waves crash on the surface. These kinds of exercises are great to use with your kids, or with yourself, to help bring you back to your hub of awareness.

Knowing how to be present, or to return to that state of calm awareness, is a wonderful ability to develop. To teach this idea to your kids, you'll want to remind them how much easier things are *for them* when they feel calm and are able to think clearly. When they get caught up in thoughts and emotions that pull them away from that state, they can end up stuck on the rim, fixated on just a few aspects of their life instead of seeing the big picture. Since that way of living isn't particularly pleasant (for anyone), you want to give your kids tools that allow them to become unstuck and to return to their hub – their natural state of open and peaceful awareness. It's only from that vantage point that they have the rational skills to solve whatever they're struggling with.

Although this exercise begins as a meditative practice, it ultimately will become something that your kids can use wherever they are – not just when they're lying in a quiet room. However, to do this the first time, find a quiet place with your child and start by guiding him through taking a few deep breaths (in through the nose and out through the mouth). You can then say something like this:

> *Continue to breathe deeply and begin to bring your attention to your body. Even if you've never noticed it before, you are now becoming aware of a deepening calm within yourself – a place where you feel peace of mind. This is your own inner center of calm and stillness. If you can, gently place your hands where you notice that feeling of calmness within your body and anchor it there for yourself.*
>
> *From this place of calm you can look out and see all the aspects of your life – not just the few things you struggle with, but also the parts of your life that bring you happiness and comfort. That calm place is the part of you that knows everything, the part of you that helps you think clearly and respond thoughtfully. That is the hub of the wheel of awareness, that place of openness and clear seeing.*
>
> *As you sit with the awareness of this center, this hub, think about what other experiences in your daily life could help bring you back to this same state of peaceful awareness. You don't need to be meditating, or even in a quiet room. Anything can bring you back to it. The sound of a bird chirping, or your dog barking, could be what brings you back to this moment. Maybe snuggling your favorite stuffed animal or the smell of mom's hair. These everyday things can grab your attention and remind you to return to this peaceful state – when you're upset, and even when you're not. The more you return, the more it becomes second nature and the easier it becomes to relax and feel peaceful and happy.*

Ask your child if he can come up with a few suggestions for what could remind him of his ability to return to this state of internal awareness. Anything could work – washing dishes, tying his shoes, the sound of a chair being moved across the classroom floor. For some kids, it's the waves of the breath, in and out. Once he's chosen, direct him to let those particular events, whenever they might occur, be a signal that his inner calm is reminding him to pay attention. Each day, ask your child to share how he was reminded to return to his hub and what he became aware of because of it.

Even if it feels a bit forced in the beginning – and even if you need to point out those reminders at first – it can ultimately become habit. At that point, the breath, the sound of a doorbell, a distant cough, even a child's laugh, can be an instant cue to shift focus to a more peaceful state of awareness. And who couldn't benefit from that?

WHOLE-BRAIN KIDS: TEACH YOUR KIDS ABOUT INTEGRATING THE MANY PARTS OF THEMSELVES

The reflections and exercises in this chapter offer a great opportunity to teach your child about mindsight and the power of focused attention. It can be a great idea to create a Wheel of Awareness with your child. Here's the Whole-Brain Kids, you can read together to get clear on the basic idea.

WHOLE-BRAIN KIDS: Teach Your Kids About Integrating the Many Parts of Themselves

CHOOSING WHAT YOU THINK ABOUT

DO YOU EVER FEEL LIKE YOU "GET STUCK" ON A FEELING OR A THOUGHT? MAYBE AN UNHAPPY ONE THAT'S SO POWERFUL IT MAKES YOU FORGET ABOUT OTHER FEELINGS AND THOUGHTS THAT MAKE YOU HAPPY OR EXCITED?

THE GOOD NEWS IS THAT YOU DON'T HAVE TO STAY STUCK ON FEELINGS THAT UPSET YOU. YOU CAN LEARN TO FOCUS ON OTHER PARTS OF YOURSELF AND GET UNSTUCK.

FOR EXAMPLE:

NASSIM COULDN'T STOP THINKING ABOUT THE SPELLING BEE. HE EVEN HAD A STOMACHACHE. HE DIDN'T FEEL LIKE EATING HIS LUNCH OR PLAYING AT RECESS. ALL HE COULD THINK ABOUT WAS SPELL-ING. HE WAS NERVOUS.

THEN HIS TEACHER, MS. ANDERSON, TAUGHT HIM ABOUT HIS WHEEL OF AWARENESS. SHE EXPLAINED THAT OUR MINDS ARE LIKE A BICYCLE WHEEL. AT THE CENTER OF THE WHEEL, CALLED THE HUB, IS OUR SAFE PLACE WHERE OUR MIND CAN RELAX AND CHOOSE WHAT IT THINKS ABOUT.

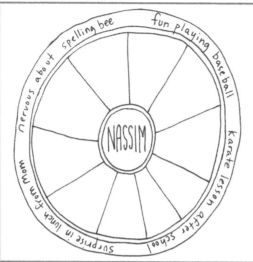

ON THE RIM OF THE WHEEL ARE ALL THE THINGS NASSIM COULD THINK ABOUT AND FEEL: HOW HE LIKES PLAYING BASE-BALL AT RECESS, WHAT SURPRISE HIS MOM COULD HAVE PACKED IN HIS LUNCH, AND, OF COURSE, HIS NERVOUSNESS ABOUT THE SPELLING BEE. SHE EX-PLAINED THAT HE WAS ONLY FOCUSING ON THE NERVOUSNESS POINT ON HIS RIM AND IGNORING THE OTHER PARTS.

MS. ANDERSON HAD NASSIM CLOSE HIS EYES AND TAKE THREE DEEP BREATHS. SHE SAID, "YOU'VE BEEN FOCUSING ON YOUR WORRIES ABOUT SPELLING. NOW I WANT YOU TO FOCUS ON THE PART OF YOUR WHEEL THAT HAS FUN PLAYING BASEBALL, AND THE PART THAT CAN IMAGINE A YUMMY LUNCH." HE SMILED AND HIS STOMACH STARTED TO GRUMBLE.

WHEN NASSIM OPENED HIS EYES HE FELT BETTER. HE HAD USED HIS WHEEL OF AWARENESS TO FOCUS ON OTHER FEELINGS AND THOUGHTS, AND HE HAD CHANGED HOW HE FELT. HE WAS STILL A LITTLE NERVOUS, BUT HE WASN'T STUCK ON <u>JUST</u> THE NERVOUSNESS.

HE LEARNED THAT HE DOESN'T HAVE TO THINK ONLY ABOUT NERVOUS FEELINGS, AND THAT HE CAN USE HIS MIND TO THINK ABOUT OTHER THINGS THAT CAN HELP HIM HAVE FUN AND NOT FEEL SO WORRIED. NASSIM ATE HIS LUNCH AND RAN OUTSIDE TO PLAY BASEBALL.

Then you can create your child's own wheel. Again, the look isn't what's important. Have your child fill in the rim-points, including unpleasant feelings and thoughts, as well as the good things in her life.

After filling in the wheel, help your child start by focusing on those negative experiences that make up her wheel (*the broken bicycle, the cancelled birthday party, having to share a room with her sister…*) and ask her to describe how she feels after spending some time concentrating on those aspects of her rim. Encourage her to SIFT and consider her current physical state, as well any images, feelings, and thoughts she may have about her life.

As you explore this exercise with your child, bring her attention to the fact that a simple shift in her focus altered her view of her world. Remind her that she has this power to change the way she feels about anything in her life, simply by choosing to shift the focus of her attention and open her awareness to something else.

PUTTING IT ALL TOGETHER: LOOKING AT OUR OWN WHEEL OF AWARENESS

There are many ways parents can benefit from an understanding of mindsight and their own wheel of awareness. Here's an exercise from *The Whole-Brain Child* that can help you see, and experience, what we're talking about.

From your hub, SIFT through your own mind. What rim–points have your attention right now? Maybe some of these?

- I'm so tired. I wish I had one more hour of sleep.

- I'm also irritated that my son's Dodgers cap is there on the floor. Now when he gets home I'll have to ride him about that *and* about his homework.

- Dinner with the Coopers will be fun tonight, but I kind of wish we weren't going.

- I'm tired.

- I wish I did more for myself. At least I'm giving myself the pleasure of reading a book these days.

- Did I mention I'm tired?

All of these sensations, images, feelings and thoughts are the rim-points on your wheel of awareness, and together they determine your state of mind.

Now let's see what happens when you intentionally direct your attention to other rim points. Slow down for a few seconds, get quiet within yourself, and ask yourself these questions:

- What's something funny or adorable my child said or did lately?

- Even though it's monstrously difficult at times, do I genuinely love and appreciate getting to be a parent? How would I feel if I didn't get to be a parent?

- What's my child's favorite T-shirt right now? Can I remember her first pair of shoes?

- Can I picture how my child might look at eighteen, bags packed, leaving for college?

Feeling different? Has your state of mind changed?

Mindsight did that. From your hub you noticed the rim-points on your own wheel of awareness, and you became aware of what you were experiencing. Then you shifted your focus, directing your attention to other rim points, and as a result, your entire state of mind changed. *This is the power of the mind, and this how it can literally and fundamentally transform the way you feel about and interact with your kids.* This is how integrating your mind—linking the different parts of your inner mental life—can be so empowering. That's the integration that mindsight creates. The Wheel of Awareness enables you to take in all the different rim elements and link them together from an open and flexible hub of your mind. Without mindsight, you can get stuck on your rim, feeling primarily frustrated or angry or resentful. The joy of parenting is gone in that moment. But by returning to your hub and shifting your focus, you can begin to experience joy and gratitude about getting to parent your children – just by paying attention and deciding to direct your attention to new rim-points.

Mindsight can also be immensely practical. For example, think for a moment right now about the last time you got angry with one of your children. Really, really angry, where you could've lost control. Remember what he did, and how furious you felt. At times like these, the anger you feel burns bright and fiery on the rim of your wheel. In fact, it burns so intensely that it pulls you out of the hub and it outshines all the other rim-points that represent the feelings and knowledge you have about your kids: your understanding that your four-year old is acting like a normal four-year old; your memory of laughing hysterically together, just a few minutes earlier, as you played cards; the promise you made that you were going to stop grabbing your children's arms when you're angry; your desire to model appropriate expressions of anger.

This is how we become swept up on the rim when we're not integrated via the hub. Another way of looking at this is that the downstairs brain takes over any integrative functioning of the upstairs area, and the other rim-points are eclipsed by the glare of this single point of your all-consuming anger. Remember "flipping your lid"?

What do you need to do in a moment like this? Yep, you guessed it: integrate. Use your mindsight skills. By focusing on your breath, you can at least begin to get back to the hub of your mind. This is the required step that allows us to pull back from being consumed by a single angry point on the rim – or a few of them. Once in the hub, it becomes possible to take in the wider perspective that there are other rim-points to keep in mind. The hub lets you SIFT and shift. You can get some water, take a break and stretch, or give yourself a moment to collect yourself. Then once you've brought your awareness back to your hub, you'll be free to choose how you want to focus your attention and how to respond to your child and if necessary repair any breach in your relationship.

This doesn't mean ignoring bad behavior. Not at all. In fact, one of the rim-points you'll integrate along with the others is your belief in setting clear and consistent boundaries. There are many perspectives you can embrace, from desires for your child to act in a different way to feelings of concern over how you acted in response. When you link all these different rim-points together – when you've used the hub to integrate your mind in the moment – you'll feel a readiness to continue attuned, sensitive parenting from this receptive and not reactive state of mind. Then, with your whole brain working together, you can connect with your child because you're connected with yourself. You'll have a much better chance of responding the way you want to, with mindsight and the wholeness of who you are, instead of an immediate reaction spurred on by a fiery point on the rim of your wheel.

CHAPTER 6

The Me-We Connection
Integrating Self and Other

*Helping children become a participating member of a "we"
while not losing touch with their individual "me" is a tall order
for any parent. But happiness and fulfillment result from being
connected to others while still maintaining a unique identity.
That's also the essence of mindsight, which is all about seeing
your own mind, as well as the mind of another. It's about
developing fulfilling relationships while maintaining
a healthy sense of self.*

— The Whole-Brain Child

While our kids may be able to do many things, seeing the world from another person's perspective is a lot for parents to expect of a young child. However, while it's important to know that much of what we want for our children will come with time, parents also need to remember that we can prepare and steer them towards becoming children, teens and, ultimately, adults who are able not only to consider the feelings of others, but also to build the type of strong, loving relationships we wish for them.

The previous chapters in this workbook were about helping your child develop his whole brain in order to build his insight and form a strong and resilient sense of "me". This chapter will focus on the interpersonal aspect of mindsight: seeing and understanding the minds of the people around us. Much of the focus will be on helping develop empathy and compassion in our kids, so they can develop abilities and strengths that will help them in relationships throughout their lives. Being able to maintain a strong sense of self, while being connected with others, is what ultimately leads to happiness and fulfillment. Achieving personal insight *while at the same time* seeing and understanding the minds of those around us is also the essence of mindsight.

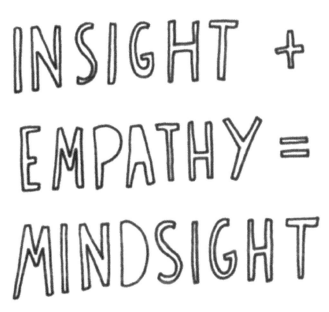

THE SOCIAL BRAIN: WIRED FOR "WE"

What scientists have discovered over the past few decades is that our brains are meant to be in relation with each other. In other words, the signals you get each day from socializing, engaging, and interacting with others influences the development of your own inner world. As we said in *The Whole-Brain Child*, "…what happens *between* brains has a great deal to do with what happens *within* each individual brain.:

Because young children are naturally focused on themselves in their early years, we need to help them move beyond that "single skull" perspective – the view that their individual brain is a lone organ isolated in a single skull – into an understanding of how they're connected to family, friends, their community and, ultimately, a world that's much bigger than themselves. In this way, the "me" discovers meaning and happiness by joining and belonging to a "we." This is another type of integration: *interpersonal integration.* In Dan's book *Brainstorm,* the term he introduces for this integrated self of "me" and "we" is "MWe". MWe is an integrated identity that honors the individual me while also honoring the importance of our interconnected lives.

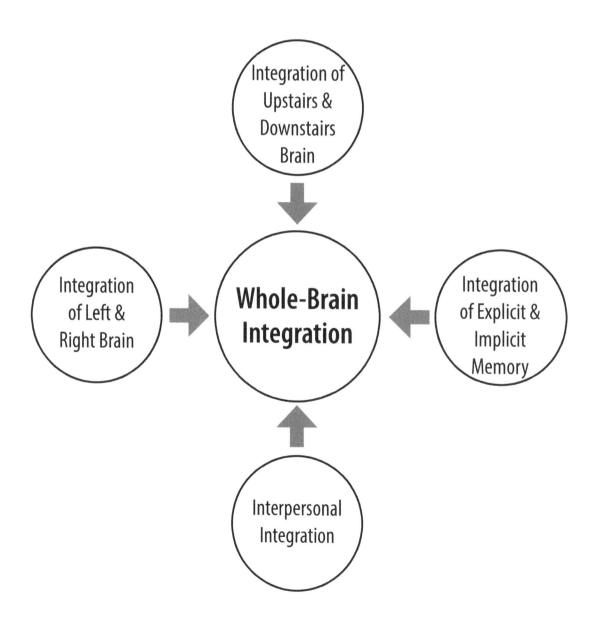

LAYING THE GROUNDWORK FOR CONNECTION: CREATING POSITIVE MENTAL MODELS

The most important people in your child's life do much more than just love her and keep her safe. These caregivers – parents, grandparents, significant babysitters, teachers, peers, and other important figures in his world – will lay the groundwork for what she understands about relationships and how she connects to others for the rest of her life.

Because the people who are most important to your child have such a profound influence on her emotional intelligence and social development, their importance can't be overestimated.

Think now about the caretakers and important people in your child's life. Take a moment to write their names down and then answer the following questions for each person: what kind of mental model is my child receiving from this person? How do I feel about it? Are there any changes I want to make – either to get my child more time with the positive models, or less with the negative ones? We've offered a few suggestions in the chart below; fill in the rest with your own details.

Name	Relationship Mental Model	My Feelings	Action
Coach Taylor	*Being in a relationship means working together and making sacrifices for others. Being a leader means being a role model – not a dictator.*	*Positive. Strong male role model who offers firm guidance with respect and kindness.*	*Ask Coach if there is a Summer program to attend, make sure my son attends practice more regularly.*
Aunt Shelly	*Being in a relationship means finding fault and being critical. Being in a relationship means feeling bad about yourself or making someone else feel worse so you feel better.*	*Negative. Not someone I want influencing or sharing her views with my child.*	*Limit how often we see her. Don't leave my children alone with her. Perhaps have a conversation with Shelly about how she's affecting us.*
Joey Thomas	*Peer relationships mean competition, jealousy, rivalry, and that everyone is my adversary.*	*Negative. Not the type of friend I want for my child. Creates a stressful environment at school. My son is now seeing competition in a negative way.*	*Talk to my son about what a real friendship looks and feels like. Help him think about who his good friends are and make a plan to invite one of them over.*

Name	Relationship Mental Model	My Feelings	Action

Keep in mind that important influencers don't have to be people that your child spends the most time with. Instead, what you'll be looking at is what sort of role each person fills for your child (*teacher, peer, mentor, confidant…*), and how much impact that person seems to have on the way your child sees herself and the world around her.

THINKING ABOUT YOUR CHILD'S SENSE OF SELF

Some kids need to learn how to join with and think about others. Other kids need to develop a stronger sense of an individual self and a willingness to be strong and stand up for themselves. Remember, an integrated experience means honoring both the individual and the relational self. When one or the other is missing from the equation, life is not integrated and we can become prone to chaos or rigidity rather than living with a sense of harmony and the flourishing that comes with the well-being of integration.

In an effort to help your kids build skills and strengthen their relational "muscles," take a moment to think about any areas in which your child might need extra support developing her sense of self. Does she need support in her individual or her relational ways of being? Does she have a tendency to lose her individual self in the needs of others? Does she assert her own views too much and not take into account the needs and feelings of others? These are integration questions exploring how the individual and the relational self experiences—the "me" and the "we"—are in balance to support the integrated identity of a MWe. Think, for example, about negative self–talk, anxiety, a level of shyness that's inhibiting, difficulty asking for what she needs, or not being able to explain her feelings. Write whatever signs you've become aware of in the space below:

_____

_____

_____

_____

_____

Next, turn your attention to anything you may have noticed that could be a sign that your child needs to build skills in terms of developing her "we" – in other words, showing the capacity to interact and relate well with others. Think, for instance, about any difficulty reading social cues, not being able to tell the difference between joking and teasing, discomfort joining in group play, trouble making and keeping friends, an inability to share, or trouble seeing things from another's point of view. Write any details you may think of in the space below:

_____

_____

_____

_____

_____

Reflecting on our children's ability to use mindsight in their daily lives allows us, as parents, to provide whatever scaffolding they may need to improve their understanding of themselves and others, and thus to enjoy successful relationships. This is how we scaffold for our child's developmental experiences their development of an integrated self.

INTEGRATING THE SELF AND THE OTHER

Now get specific about how you'd like to address your child's needs in the areas you listed above. For example, if you'd describe your child as being shy, she may need encouragement to try new things, and at the same time need a parent who knows when not to push and can instead be understanding. (We refer to this as the "pushin' and cushion" method, a term Tina got from someone in one of her workshops. Some kids need more pushin', and some need more cushion. You can decide what's needed in any given moment based on your child's temperament, developmental age, mood, etc.)

On the other hand, a child who seems a good deal less able to consider the perspective of others could benefit from questions like, *"how do you think she feels?"* to help him practice his empathy. And the boisterous child might need help with reading social cues.

However you would describe your child's particular needs in terms of developing a successful "we" with others, use the lines below to detail a few specific ways you can help your child build skills in needed areas and further develop relational "muscles."

_____

_____

_____

_____

_____

Just as we don't want our kids to be only left-brained or right-brained, we also don't want them to be focused only on their individual selves – leaving them self-absorbed and isolated. Nor do we want them to be only relational – leaving them without a clear sense of their own individuality, and vulnerable to unhealthy relationships. What we do want is for them to be whole-brained, and to enjoy integrated relationships, where they are both differentiated (separate) and linked (in connection with others). That's a MWe.

CULTIVATING A "YES" STATE OF MIND: HELPING KIDS BE RECEPTIVE TO RELATIONSHIPS

You've probably noticed that there are times when your child is completely *receptive* to what you have to say, and other times when he's just *reactive*. All of us have moments where we're open to ideas, people, and experiences...and moments when we're not. When you're not feeling so open, you might actually feel shut down, closed off, and defensive. A time like that is probably *not* the best moment for your spouse to bring up the fact that you were late getting the kids to karate yesterday!

Reactive State – "No" State of Mind	Receptive State – "Yes" State of Mind
Shuts down	Listens well and feels connected
Feels defensive	Considers others' feelings
Accuses/judges	Gives the benefit of the doubt
Responds in a closed-minded manner	Feels relaxed and open
Reacts without thinking	Pauses and gives thoughtful response
Tenses muscles and increases heart rate	Relaxes muscles and slows heart rate

To help you experience within yourself these different states of mind, practice Dan's exercise we mentioned in *The Whole-Brain Child*. Enlist an adult to help you, then have your partner repeat a word several times. Your job is simply to notice what it feels like in your body as you hear the word.

The first word is "no," said firmly – and slightly harshly – seven times, with about two seconds in between each "no." Then, after another pause, your partner will say a clear – but somewhat gentler – "yes" seven times.

Write about how your body felt first when your partner said "no," (*stifling, angering, shut down, scolded...*) and then how it felt when you heard the word "yes" (*light, calm, peaceful...*).

_____

_____

_____

_____

_____

_____

These two different responses – the "no" feelings and the "yes" feelings – demonstrate what we mean when we talk about reactivity and receptivity. Reactivity emerges from our downstairs brain and leaves us feeling shut down, upset, and defensive, while a receptive state turns on the social engagement system of the upstairs brain that connects us to others, allowing us to feel safe and seen.

CREATING RECEPTIVITY IN YOUR CHILD

Now that you have a clear sense of how it feels when you're in a reactive or receptive state, let's use this knowledge to take a look at whether you've been trying to teach your kids when they're actually capable of learning!

Begin by listing below a few interactions with your child where your goal was to teach (*help, offer advice, share insight, correct behavior*). In the next two columns, describe your child's response to that teaching and then the clues that tell you whether she was in a receptive or reactive state at the time (now that you think back on it). In the final column write down your ideas for what you could do differently next time or what might have made the interaction so successful. We've offered two examples below. See if you can fill in the rest of the chart with your own experiences.

Event	Child's Response	Reactive or Receptive?	Next Time
Driving in car with my two children who are fighting. In the midst of it, I try to correct my daughter's tone of voice (in an attempt to help her get her point across without angering her brother).	Starts to cry and says I always take her brother's side. Gets even angrier with him. Crosses her arms, pouts, and turns away from me. The fighting between them continues.	Reactive. The argument between them was getting heated. Her raised voice and rigid body language were signs that she was already overwhelmed trying to defend herself against her brother — my jumping in just sent her over the edge.	Pull the car over. If possible, get them out of the car so they can have some space from each other. At the very least, address the issue later, when she's calm (and when her brother isn't with her), so she can take in the information without feeling defensive.
My son was struggling with his homework and getting very upset. I wanted to help and started by empathizing with how hard the work seemed and how frustrated he sounded. Then I asked if there was anything he needed from me.	I noticed that the empathizing helped him relax his body — his face softened, he took in a deep breath, and he sat back in his chair and sighed. When I asked if he needed anything from me he was able to talk about what was bothering him.	Receptive. I began by empathizing which allowed him to relax and take in everything else.	Sometimes I forget the empathy part and jump in with suggestions on how to fix what he's upset about. That almost never works. I need a reminder to always start by helping him feel that I understand his experience. (Connect and Redirect!)

Now that you've looked at these previous moments with your child – and given thought to how your words were received depending on her emotional state – you may find it helpful as you go forward to jot down the behaviors you notice as she moves between being reactive (*heavy sighs, rolling eyes, crossed arms…*) and receptive (*relaxed body, eye contact, making light conversation…*). You can do that in the space below:

_____

_____

_____

_____

_____

_____

Having a clear sense of how your child signals that she's in a receptive or reactive state can help you understand what she may need in that moment.

Whole-Brain Strategy #11:
Increase the Family Fun Factory – Making a Point to Enjoy Each Other

Laughter, being silly, and having fun with your kids is one simple way of switching the mood when everyone is feeling overly reactive. Of course children need boundaries and structure, but "playful parenting" and positive experiences as a family add more to your child's life and development than you may be aware of:

- Prepares children for relationships

- Encourages connection with others

- Offers positive reinforcement about being in a loving relationship

- Reinforces positive and healthy desires as dopamine is released from the reward system in connection with enjoying family relationships (i.e., fun and play is a reward)

- Reinforces bonds between parent and child

- Improves sibling relationships

- Helps to shift negative emotions

- Improves child's receptivity, reduces reactivity

- Reduces power struggles and encourages cooperation!

STRATEGY #11

INSTEAD OF COMMAND AND DEMAND...

...TRY PLAYFUL PARENTING

As adults we're often caught up with the goal of getting things done, or moving on to the next task. Because of that, teaching important life skills through play, or shifting emotions by being silly, isn't always our natural inclination. However, the more we do it, the easier it becomes. And it often saves us a lot of time and energy, because kids are more likely to cooperate when we're being playful.

CONSIDER THE POWER OF PLAYFULNESS

Think about the parts of your day that typically seem to result in power struggles between you and your child. Are there certain areas where you feel like you're pulling teeth to get your child to cooperate? For some families, getting ready to get out the door, homework time, mealtimes, or bedtime can be moments of tension and frustration – they may even have become moments you dread!

Consider the power of playfulness during times like this. How can you use silliness (or playfulness) when faced with those parts of your day that most often result in tears or tantrums? Take a look at the chart below where we've given a couple of examples of typical situations and possible alternatives. Next, add examples from your own family's experience and consider how the results might differ when you try a different response to your child's behavior or change the way you encourage her cooperation.

Situation	How I usually respond/try to get cooperation	Something silly, fun, or playful I can do instead
My son struggles to get out of the house for school each day. I feel like I'm always nagging him to do even the simplest tasks and we both end up so frustrated with each other.	Nagging (asking multiple times for each step). Chore boards. Doing everything myself. Getting irritated when at last the minute he runs back to the house for forgotten homework, sweater, lunch, etc.	• Since he loves video games, maybe I can make his morning routine into a game where each chore/responsibility done means he gets to a new level. Respond to each level reached with silly song & dance (it would probably help me reduce my stress level as well). • See if he can beat his score each week by doing things faster? Adding more responsibilities?
My daughter refuses every time she needs to take a bath. No matter how long it's been, she tries to negotiate her way out of it. I think it's more about the transition away from what she's doing – as opposed to the actual bath (she loves it once she's there).	I've tried rewards, "making deals," yelling, letting her make the schedule, etc. Now I anticipate the struggle and get annoyed before I even tell her it's time to bathe.	• Announce bath time in a silly accent or pretend I'm a character from a TV show she likes – continue with the accent throughout bath time. • Create a treasure map to lead her to the bath? • Let her ride on my back to the bathroom and pretend I'm her pony?

Situation	How I usually respond/try to get cooperation	Something silly, fun, or playful I can do instead

As busy people, it's easy to get caught up in our own agenda of wanting to get things done so we can get on to the next activity. In doing this though, we lose sight of the fact that our children are people who have their own internal lives, their own temperaments, and even their own agendas! Yes, we all need our children to learn how to cooperate, to follow through, and to think as part of the group. But losing your connection (and your patience) with your child over your desire for her to do what you want, when you want it, isn't an effective way to teach those skills.

When you face potential power struggles with your child, observe your own patterns of behavior, then make room for a different, more lighthearted response that can lead to less resistance from your child, as well as more connection between the two of you.

THINKING ABOUT OUR FAMILY'S FUN FACTOR

Of course we all have busy lives, and responsibilities outside of family time are often very important. But if you ever feel like the bulk of your time with your kids is spent correcting behavior – or just "managing" them until you can make it to bedtime – stop and ask yourself, "How much fun are we having together as a family"? If the answer to that falls into the category of "not enough," how do you think you could be more intentional about enjoying your time with your kids? What could you do so that having fun with them is at the front of your awareness more often? Consider those questions and write your thoughts here:

_____

_____

_____

_____

_____

_____

Now think about that question from the perspective of your kids. What do you think they would say about how they feel about family time? Would they say they got a boost of dopamine – a sense of excitement, pleasure, or interest – when the family is together? Do they get excited about family time? Do you think they'd say that there's more tension and fighting than fun? Will they grow up knowing that, even though no one was perfect and even though there was conflict at times, you had plenty of fun together as a family? Think about these questions and write your thoughts below:

_____

_____

_____

_____

_____

_____

Remember, family fun doesn't mean only big events. Bedtime snuggles, fort building, even laughing at corny jokes together can all be moments that bring your family together and help your children build those relationship skills we mentioned earlier. List some of the specific ways your family has fun together.

_____

_____

_____

_____

_____

Now that you've done that, take a look at all the things you listed, and take a minute to appreciate how much fun your family already has when they're together. Next, brainstorm some ideas of other ways you can bring even more fun and laughter into your family time. It might have to do with setting up a weekly game night, or getting out a joke book your kids love at dinner, or going for a bike ride, or buying tickets to the circus that's in town. Just brainstorm some ideas for increasing the family fun factor.

_____

_____

_____

_____

_____

Whole-Brain Strategy #12:
Connection Through Conflict – Teach Kids to Argue with a "We" in Mind

It's almost never fun when our kids don't get along with each other. However, if we can look at their conflicts as an opportunity to help them get better at being in relationships and develop mindsight skills, we might feel less anxious about those quarrels and disagreements when they do occur.

In *The Whole-Brain Child* we detailed three mindsight-building tools:

1. **See Through the Other Person's Eyes:** *helping kids recognize other points of view.*

2. **Listen to What's Not Being Said:** *teaching kids about nonverbal communication and attuning to others.*

3. **Repair:** *teaching kids to make things right after a conflict.*

Let's look now at how we can put these skills into action so we can all survive those individual conflicts, as well as help our kids thrive as they move toward adulthood.

SEEING THROUGH THE EYES OF ANOTHER

When our children are upset with someone often it's because they're having difficulty seeing the interaction from the other person's perspective.

STRATEGY #12
INSTEAD OF DISMISS AND DENY...

...TRY CONNECTION THROUGH CONFLICT

Because this is a skill that doesn't come naturally – especially to young children – a very literal exercise can be helpful.

It's probably easiest to try the following exercise for the first time with a conflict between your child and another family member, but you can do it with anyone you have a clear photo of.

You'll need a photo of the person your child is upset with (it could even be you!) – preferably one where the person is facing the camera – that is enlarged so that the face is approximately life-size. You'll also need scissors or an Exacto knife, two 12" pieces of yarn or string, and some clear tape.

To begin with, trim away any extra paper from the face and use the scissors or knife to cut away the eyes from the photo so you can see through them. Tape one end of each string on each the side of the mask at about temple level so you can tie them together behind your child's head like a mask.

Have your child stand in front of a mirror so she can see that not only does she look like the person she's having trouble with (*her friend, her sister, her dad...*), but she's also now literally looking out of someone else's eyes. (It's fine to have fun and even be silly during this exercise; it will feel foreign to both of you, so let yourselves enjoy it.)

While continuing to look at her masked self in the mirror, have her think about how the other person may have felt thought, both before and after the conflict.

As she does this, begin to talk about whatever she and that person have been struggling with. Your child may feel silly at first, but encourage her to continue. By taking the part of your child, you can guide the conversation and give voice to what she might have wanted to say in the moment – clarifying for her what she may have been feeling. This can allow her to begin seeing things from someone else's view. It could go something like this, if your daughter had gotten angry with one of her school friends:

> **You (playing the role of your child):** *Yesterday when I wanted to play with Lilah you made me feel like I had to play with you, or you wouldn't be my friend anymore!*
>
> **Child (wearing mask, looking in mirror, and playing the role of the other person):** *You never play with me! Anyway, you're my friend, not hers!*
>
> **You:** *Of course I'm your friend. And I always will be – even if I play with other people. When you said you wouldn't be my friend anymore that scared me.*
>
> **Child:** *Well...I didn't mean to scare you. I just wanted you to play with me. I guess...I guess I felt jealous.*
>
> **You:** *Were you scared I wouldn't be your friend anymore if I play with Lilah?*
>
> **Child:** *Yeah...maybe. Maybe I thought you would like her better than me and then I wouldn't have you as my best friend anymore?*
>
> **You:** *That must have been a really yucky feeling. I bet you got really mad and scared and worried all at the same time! It's hard for me to be calm when I feel like that and sometimes I just say the first thing I can think of! Is that kind of what happened to you?*
>
> **Child:** *Yeah...I think so. I think maybe I just wanted you to stay with me and so I said I wouldn't be your friend. I think I knew it wasn't nice, but I kind of didn't know what else to say.*

Once you feel your child has made some good guesses as to what the other person may have been feeling, you can stop the role-playing and sum things up together: *So maybe Zoe wasn't trying to be mean and bossy, maybe she was actually jealous and scared, huh? Does that make you think differently about the situation?*

Don't feel pressure to make this go perfectly. You're simply trying to get your daughter to see the situation from a different perspective.

READING NONVERBAL CUES

When it comes to relationship conflicts, in addition to seeing things from more than one point of view, it's essential to be able to understand someone's body language, facial expressions, and tone of voice. These nonverbal clues sometimes communicate even more than words, and because kids aren't naturally skilled at interpreting what's *not* being said, we need to help them. Sometimes this is just about raising the issue for your kids, which may go like this:

> **Dad:** *How's Matt taking the loss?*
>
> **Son:** *I just talked to him. He said he's fine.*
>
> **Dad:** *Look at him over there. Do you believe him? Does he look like he's taking it OK?*
>
> **Son:** *Maybe not.*
>
> **Dad:** *Want to go say hey again?*
>
> **Son:** *Yeah, all right.*

Sometimes it requires more work on your part and you'll need to point out the many ways people communicate. There are a few simple ways to do this, but let's start first by writing about how good you think your child is at reading nonverbal cues. What sort of nonverbal cues is he good at picking up? Are there any reasons you think he's better at recognizing some and less aware of others? Explore these questions here.

_____

_____

_____

_____

_____

_____

_____

_____

_____

_____

These reflections will help you pinpoint your child's strengths, as well as where he needs to develop skills when it comes to noticing and understanding the subtleties of communication. Even children who are pretty socially savvy can sometimes use extra help deciphering what's really going on in their relationships.

READ MY CUES: A GUESSING GAME

One way to increase your child's empathy and insight is by playing a guessing game called Read My Cues. For preschoolers, you can begin by demonstrating different emotions with your face and body and asking your child to guess the feeling. You can have them show you as well: "Show me what your body and face look like when you are happy. Now show me mad."

Then, when kids are school age, you can begin by telling your child that in addition to what they say, all people send signals – or – cues about what they are feeling in a number of other ways. For example, a child who has just lost a big soccer game may say he's fine, but his drooping shoulders, lowered head, and downcast face are nonverbal cues that say otherwise.

Using pictures around your house, magazines, or photo albums, have your child describe what he thinks each person is feeling by looking at the body language and facial expressions. You can expand this game by doing the same exercise using a movie or television program with the sound turned off, or even in a public place – as long as you're not so close that people know you're talking about them!

In the therapy office, we've used poster boards and divided each side of the posters into four squares and labeled them with different feelings. We use the posters in various ways, such as having the child stand on the squares and act out the feeling, having them cut out pictures from magazines and glue them onto the appropriate box, or even draw their own face feeling these emotions. You could take a picture of your child acting out various emotions and labeling them to go into a book as well. There are lots of ways to do this! Get creative!

Then, the next time your child experiences a conflict with a friend, or is confused about someone's behavior, bring them back to one of these activities and ask them to think about what nonverbal communication they might have missed that could give them clues about how to solve the situation.

LEARNING TO REPAIR

As adults, we know the importance of saying "I'm sorry," and we teach our children to recognize moments when they need to apologize. But children also need to know when repair is in order, and when they need to take steps to correct a mistake they've made. When we're able to break through our children's defensiveness and reluctance to accept responsibility, we can help them be thoughtful about others they've hurt, and guide them in making an effort toward reconnection.

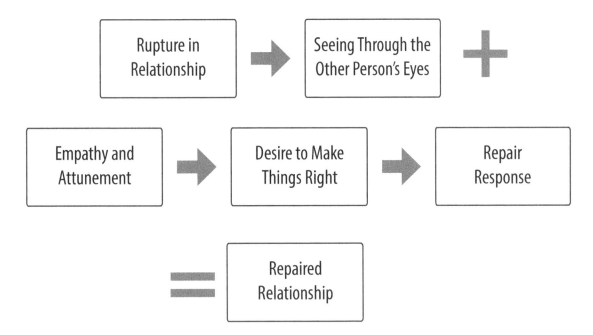

Let's take a look at a recent conflict between your child and someone else—maybe a friend or a sibling. How did you help your child develop mindsight and consider the other person's feelings? Was anything done to make it right? If so, was it a specific, direct response (like replacing a broken toy) or a more relational response (like writing an apology letter or doing something kind for the other person)? How did your child feel about performing the repair? If no repair was made, has the relationship been affected? What, if anything, would you do differently next time? Write your thoughts here:

_____

_____

_____

_____

_____

_____

_____

As with many of the other skills we've discussed in this workbook, modeling the ability to make a repair goes a long way toward teaching it. If you've experienced a rupture with your child when maybe you lost your temper, were impatient, or said something in a way you wish you hadn't, show your child that you, too, can make a sincere and heartfelt apology. Children do as we do. Actions speak louder than words.

WHOLE-BRAIN KIDS: TEACH YOUR KIDS ABOUT INTEGRATING THE SELF WITH THE OTHER

In addition to the exercises we've suggested, the cartoon below was created so you could read it with your child to help introduce the concept of seeing your own and each other's minds.

WHOLE BRAIN KIDS: Teach Your Kids About Integrating the Self with Others

ME AND WE

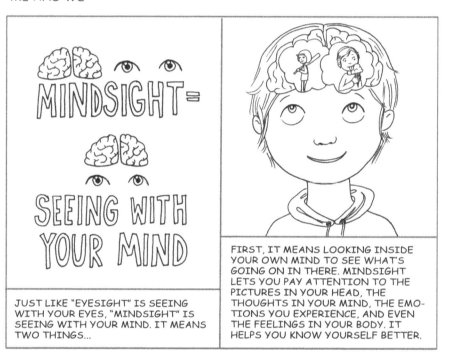

MINDSIGHT = SEEING WITH YOUR MIND

JUST LIKE "EYESIGHT" IS SEEING WITH YOUR EYES, "MINDSIGHT" IS SEEING WITH YOUR MIND. IT MEANS TWO THINGS...

FIRST, IT MEANS LOOKING INSIDE YOUR OWN MIND TO SEE WHAT'S GOING ON IN THERE. MINDSIGHT LETS YOU PAY ATTENTION TO THE PICTURES IN YOUR HEAD, THE THOUGHTS IN YOUR MIND, THE EMOTIONS YOU EXPERIENCE, AND EVEN THE FEELINGS IN YOUR BODY. IT HELPS YOU KNOW YOURSELF BETTER.

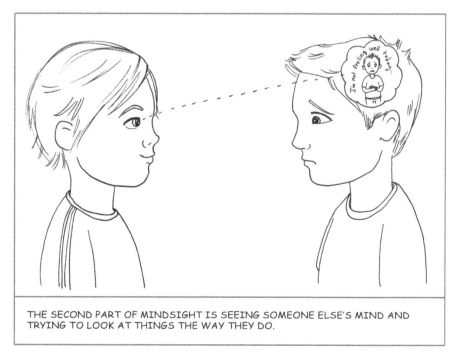

THE SECOND PART OF MINDSIGHT IS SEEING SOMEONE ELSE'S MIND AND TRYING TO LOOK AT THINGS THE WAY THEY DO.

FOR EXAMPLE:

DREW CAME HOME FROM A PLAYDATE AND TOLD HIS DAD THAT HE AND TIM HAD ARGUED OVER WHO GOT TO USE TIM'S NEW WATER GUN. THEY HAD EVENTUALLY DECIDED TO TAKE TURNS, BUT WHEN DREW GOT HOME, HE STILL FELT ANGRY.

HE EXPLAINED THAT SINCE HE WAS THE GUEST, HE FELT THAT TIM SHOULD HAVE LET HIM USE THE NEW WATER GUN. DREW'S DAD LISTENED AND SAID HE UNDERSTOOD. THEN HE ASKED, "WHY DO YOU THINK TIM WANTED TO USE IT SO MUCH?"

DREW THOUGHT FOR A SECOND. "BECAUSE IT WAS NEW, AND HE HADN'T GOTTEN TO PLAY WITH IT YET?" IN THAT MOMENT, DREW USED HIS MINDSIGHT TO UNDERSTAND TIM'S FEELINGS. HE DIDN'T FEEL AS MAD ANYMORE.

THE NEXT TIME YOU'RE UPSET WITH SOMEONE, USE YOUR OWN MINDSIGHT TO SEE HOW THE OTHER PERSON FEELS. IT CAN MAKE YOU BOTH FEEL A LOT HAPPIER.

Any step you can take that builds mindsight skills like insight and empathy in your kids will be a significant gift you give them, and an investment in their future relational success.

INTEGRATING OURSELVES: MAKING SENSE OF OUR OWN STORY

Now that we've spent some time reading and thinking about how your child can improve his relationship skills, let's turn the focus back to you, the parent. How well we've made sense of our experiences with our own parents and how sensitive we are to our children is what most powerfully influences our relationship with our kids, and therefore how well they thrive.

It all comes down to what we call our **life narrative,** the story we tell when we look at who we are and how we've become the person that we are. Our life narrative reveals:

- Our feelings about our past

- Our understanding of why people (like our parents) behaved as they did

- Our awareness of the way those events have impacted our development into adulthood.

As we've discussed throughout this workbook, when we learn how not to parent reactively we can instead be responsive to what our children most need in the moment. Reactive parenting occurs, in great part, when we haven't examined our life narrative because unresolved hurts, unmet needs, and our beliefs from the past intrude upon the present – sometimes even without our awareness.

For example, consider how experiences, behaviors, and coping strategies that aren't examined, can affect generations of people in a family.

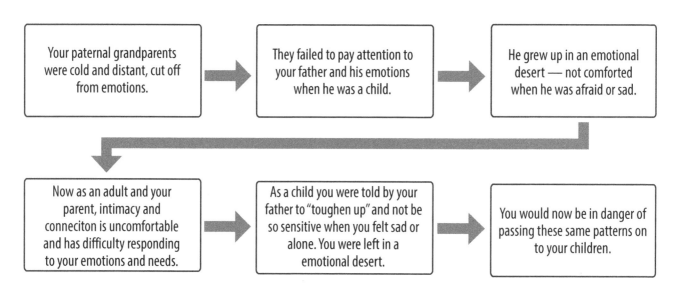

The good news though, is that if you reflect on your own story and understand and make sense of your experiences and your parents' limitations, you can break the cycle of handing down this sort of pain. A difficult childhood doesn't condemn you to being a bad parent. In fact, by making sense of your life narrative it's possible even to turn past suffering into your parenting strengths. (If you'd like to explore this idea more deeply, Dan and Mary Hartzell wrote a whole book that examines these concepts in great detail: *Parenting From the Inside Out.*)

UNDERSTANDING YOUR LIFE NARRATIVE

Regardless of our childhood, we all adopt strategies that help us cope with our life experiences. Sometimes these behaviors work to our advantage:

> *As a way of coping with a chaotic childhood environment, Tim became very organized. This skill helps him successfully manage a busy corporation.*

However, sometimes the way people deal with early experiences can also end up limiting them:

> *Tim's skill at organization is also a need. He uses it to control the stress he feels when things don't go as planned. Disorganization leaves him feeling anxious and unable to adjust his thinking. In order to avoid that, he resorts to over-planning every step of the day and can be rigid and inflexible toward his employees.*

When you openly reflect on your childhood experiences and how life with your parents may have affected you – for better or worse – you're giving yourself the opportunity to understand yourself in deeper and much more meaningful ways. As a result, you'll be able to attune to your own children in the way they most need it, and to set them up for having their own childhood experiences that encourage (among many other things) social, emotional, and intellectual growth.

For the workbook's closing reflection, we want to give you a chance to think about your own childhood, and how you were parented. In the space below, write about the positive memories you have of your relationship with your parents. What did they do well in terms of making you feel loved? How did they show you consistent, nurturing care you could count on? Think about how they expressed that they were interested in you, how you knew you were understood and accepted by them, and what they did to create a safe place for you to express yourself. Write your thoughts here:

_____
_____
_____
_____
_____
_____
_____
_____
_____

Now write about what your parents could have done better. In what ways did you feel that you didn't have their attention, or that their love wasn't always available, or that you were only accepted on their terms? Do your best to be honest about your parents' shortcomings. Recognizing where your parents may have let you down doesn't mean you're saying they were bad people; what you're doing here is allowing yourself to shine the light of awareness on labels, thoughts, and impressions you have about yourself and your life. Although you may not have been fully conscious of these ideas, it's possible that they affect you, nevertheless. Write whatever memories and thoughts you have about this here:

_____

_____

_____

_____

_____

_____

The last part of this reflection is to do your best to understand where these shortcomings came from. *Why* were your parents unable to give you all that you needed, emotionally and relationally? Were they too busy (*with work, with other children, with health problems…*)? Had they been wounded themselves? Did they not have the knowledge or support to get the parenting tools they needed?

You aren't looking for excuses for their behavior, any more than you're looking for reasons to judge. As you think and write, do your best to simply observe what you notice. Emotions will likely come up, and that's fine. You'll want to deal with those at some point. But for the moment, as much as you can, just observe what you see about your parents without judging. You're simply looking for a sense of understanding and explanation for who your parents were, and why they parented you the way they did.

_____

_____

_____

_____

_____

Working through this exercise – and, really, this entire workbook – is the beginning of being able to separate triggering memories and unresolved past emotions from your childhood, from what's happening in the present moment with your own child. Once you can do this, you are steps closer to not only releasing the burden of those memories, but also being able to be the parent you truly want to be, and the one your child needs.

We want to make this point as clearly as possible: early experience is not fate. By making sense of your past you can free yourself from what might otherwise be a cross-generational legacy of pain and insecure attachment, and instead create an inheritance of predictable, sensitive care and love for your children, a relationship in which they feel safe, secure, seen, and soothed.

Knowing that our kids live with – and through – whatever we're experiencing is a powerful insight that can motivate us to begin and continue our journey toward understanding our own stories, the joys as well as the pain. We can then attune to the needs and signals of our children, creating secure attachment and strong and healthy connection.

Bringing It All Together

*It's extraordinary when you think about the generational impact
of Whole-Brain parenting. Do you realize the power you now
have to effect positive change in the future? By giving your
children the gift of using their whole brain, you're impacting
not just their lives, but also those of all the
people with whom they interact.*

– The Whole-Brain Child

We want to close this workbook with one last visualization that we hope will inspire you to continue on the road towards intentionality and integration.

Take a moment right now and, with your eyes closed, imagine your child as an adult. Be as specific as possible, imagining as many details (face shape, body, hair color, eyes ...) as you can.

Now imagine that adult—your child grown up—holding your grandchild. What kind of parent will your child be? Patient? Respectful? Kind? Present? In other words, what will you have modeled for your child, and what kind of expectations will you have set up with the way you have parented? Write about that now.

_____

_____

_____

_____

_____

_____

_____

_____

_____

We offer this visualization *not* to put pressure on you, but to point out how exciting it is that you're making this effort to be a self-aware, connected parent. By doing the difficult work of examining your own parenting style and thinking about how best to raise your own children, you're offering your future grandchildren an important gift by facilitating integration in your own children. You're connecting with them before redirecting. You're teaching them to name their fears so they can tame them. You're showing them how to focus their attention so they can take control of their own emotions and actions. In doing all of this, you're offering them a legacy that will significantly impact future generations.

But let us say it again: you're not perfect. And you won't be perfect. Ever. Neither are we when we parent our own children. Our job is not to avoid making mistakes, any more than it is to protect our kids from experiencing difficult moments. Our job is to connect with our children, and to walk with them through the hard times. As we say in *The Whole-Brain Child*, "The beauty of Whole-Brain Parenting is that it lets you understand that *even the mistakes are opportunities* to grow and learn. This approach involves being intentional about what we're doing and where we're going, even while accepting that we are all human. Intention and attention are our goals, not some rigid, harsh expectation of perfection."

So don't put pressure on yourself. Have fun with your kids, and be willing to apologize and repair when conflict arises. Keep in mind that even those moments when you're just trying to survive until bedtime, you can use your interactions with your children to help them thrive. To help them be happier, healthier, and more fully themselves. What a gift to offer not only your kids and your family, but the world itself.

With those ideals in mind, we want to give you the last word. In the space below, choose one or two areas you'd like to work on right now to be more intentional with your parenting. Perhaps page through the workbook, looking at your answers to the questions we've asked. Based on what you see, write about a couple of steps you can take right now to help you be the kind of parent you want to be—for your kids, and for yourself.

_____

_____

_____

_____

_____

_____

_____

_____

_____

_____

_____

_____

_____

ACKNOWLEDGMENTS

We want to begin by thanking all of you who have loved The Whole-Brain Child and infused it into your family and professional lives. We didn't originally intend to write a companion workbook for The Whole-Brain Child. But so many of you connected with us and asked for ways to go deeper into the Whole-Brain ideas, to have additional tools to use in groups or book clubs or parent education classes, that we wanted to respond. So thank you for your requests, and for how you have embraced The Whole-Brain Child.

In addition, we thank our students, along with the colleagues and parents and children we've worked with individually and in groups and in our offices, for helping us hone these ideas and find ways to turn theory and science into practice. The stories you've shared and the questions you've asked have helped us clarify and deepen our understanding of the ideas we're so passionate about.

We also want to thank PESI for being so supportive throughout the whole publication process. We especially appreciate Linda Jackson, our publisher. She communicated her enthusiasm from the very beginning and was responsive and professional, providing everything we needed. She's been a delight to work with.

Finally, we thank Gina Osher, without whose contributions this book wouldn't have been written. Her creativity and insights were invaluable to us, and her influence on the writing of The Whole-Brain Child Workbook can't be overstated.

We hope this book offers even more opportunities for parents and other caregivers to interact with the kids they love in ways that help them grow to be happier, healthier, and more fully themselves.

Dan and Tina

ABOUT THE AUTHORS

 **Daniel J. Siegel, M.D.** is a graduate of Harvard Medical School and completed his postgraduate medical education at UCLA with training in pediatrics and child, adolescent, and adult psychiatry. He is currently a clinical professor of psychiatry at the UCLA School of Medicine, founding co-director of UCLA's Mindful Awareness Research Center, co-investigator at the UCLA Center for Culture, Brain and Development, and executive director of the Mindsight Institute.

Dr. Siegel's psychotherapy practice spans 25 years and he has published extensively for the professional audience. Dr. Siegel's books include Mindsight, Pocket Guide to Interpersonal Neurobiology, *The Developing Mind, Second Edition, The Mindful Therapist, The Mindful Brain, Parenting from the Inside Out* (with Mary Hartzell, M.Ed.), and the three *New York Times* bestsellers: *Brainstorm, The Whole-Brain Child* (with Tina Payne Bryson, Ph.D.), and his latest *No-Drama Discipline* (with Tina Payne Bryson, Ph.D.). He has been invited to lecture for the King of Thailand, Pope John Paul II, His Holiness the Dalai Lama, Google University, and TEDx.

Dr. Tina Payne Bryson is the co-author (with Dan Siegel) of two *New York Times* bestsellers: *Whole-Brain Child* and *No-Drama Discipline.* She is a pediatric and adolescent psychotherapist, the Director of Parenting for the Mindsight Institute, and the Child Development Specialist at Saint Mark's School in Altadena, CA. She keynotes conferences and conducts workshops for parents, educators, and clinicians all over the world. Dr. Bryson earned her Ph.D. from the University of Southern California, and she lives near Los Angeles with her husband and three children. You can learn more about her at TinaBryson.com, where you can subscribe to her blog and read her articles about kids and parenting.